THE CONTINUATION OF SOMETHING

Great

Jesus' Teaching and Training of the Disciples
A Study of Luke 7:1–10:37

BIBLE STUDY GUIDE

From the Bible-teaching ministry of

Charles R. Swindoll

INSIGHT FOR LIVING

Chuck graduated in 1963 from Dallas Theological Seminary, where he now serves as the school's fourth president, helping to prepare a new generation of men and women for the ministry. Chuck has served in pastorates in three states: Massachusetts, Texas, and California, including almost twenty-three years at the First Evangelical Free Church in Fullerton, California. His sermon messages have been aired over radio since 1979 as the *Insight for Living* broadcast. A best-selling author, Chuck has written numerous books and booklets on many subjects.

Based on the outlines and transcripts of Chuck's sermons, the study guide text is co-authored by Bryce Klabunde, a graduate of Biola University and Dallas Theological Seminary. He also wrote the Living Insights sections.

Editor in Chief:
Cynthia Swindoll

Coauthor of Text:
Bryce Klabunde

Assistant Editor:
Wendy Peterson

Copy Editors:
Deborah Gibbs
Glenda Schlahta
Karene Wells

Editorial Assistant:
Nancy Hubbard

Text Designer:
Gary Lett

Publishing System Specialist:
Bob Haskins

Director, Communications and Marketing Division:
Deedee Snyder

Marketing Manager:
Alene Cooper

Project Coordinator:
Colette Muse

Production Manager:
John Norton

Printer:
Sinclair Printing Company

Unless otherwise identified, all Scripture references are from the New American Standard Bible, © The Lockman Foundation 1960, 1962, 1963, 1968, 1971, 1972, 1973, 1975, 1977. Used by permission. Scripture taken from the Holy Bible, New International Version © 1973, 1978, 1984 International Bible Society, used by permission of Zondervan Bible Publishers. The other translation cited is the *New King James Version* [NKJV].

ISBN 0-8499-8623-0
COVER DESIGN: Gary Lett
COVER PAINTING: *The Storm on the Sea of Galilee* by Rembrandt van Rijn
Printed in the United States of America

CONTENTS

INTRODUCTION

In this section of Luke's gospel, we'll see Jesus accelerating His training program for the Twelve as He sets His face toward Jerusalem and the Cross. He uses every possible situation to equip His men to carry on His work after He's gone.

He'll teach them about faith during a raging storm,
about compassion through a grieving widow,
about real love with a shunned prostitute.

When He feeds the multitudes with the loaves and fishes, His disciples will hand out the food. When He displays His glory on the Mount of Transfiguration, Peter, James, and John will be watching in amazement.

Every teachable moment will make an indelible impression on the minds of His followers.

As Christ continues doing something great in you, let Him equip you as His disciples through these stories from Luke. Let Him open your heart to the teachable moments in your life.

Chuck Swindoll

Chuck Swindoll

PUTTING TRUTH
INTO ACTION

K nowledge apart from application falls short of God's desire for His children. He wants us to apply what we learn so that we will change and grow. This study guide was prepared with these goals in mind. As you go through the following pages, we hope your desire to discover biblical truth will grow as your understanding of God's Word increases and that you will be encouraged to apply what you've learned.

To assist you in your study, we've included a section called Living Insights at the end of each lesson. These exercises will challenge you to study further and to think of specific ways to put your discoveries into action.

On occasion a lesson is followed by a Digging Deeper section, which gives you additional information and resources to probe further into some issues raised in that lesson.

There are many ways to use this guide—in personal devotions, group studies, discussions with friends and family, and Sunday school classes. And, of course, it's an ideal study aid when you're listening to its corresponding *Insight for Living* radio series.

To benefit most from this study guide, we would encourage you to consider it a spiritual journal. That's why we've included space in the **Living Insights** for recording your thoughts and discoveries. We hope you'll return to those sections often for review and encouragement as you continue to grow in your walk with Christ.

Bryce Klabunde
Coauthor of Text
Author of Living Insights

THE CONTINUATION OF SOMETHING

Great

Jesus' Teaching and Training of the Disciples
A Study of Luke 7:1–10:37

LUKE: A PHYSICIAN'S OPINION

Writer: Luke, a Gentile Christian physician (first mentioned in Acts 16:10)

Date: Around A.D. 60

Style: Scholarly, detailed, people-oriented

Appeal: Directly to Greeks, but universal

Message: Jesus is truly human

Key Phrase: "The Son of Man" (Luke 19:10)

Interesting Facts:

- This is the only gospel account specifically addressed to an individual: "most excellent Theophilus" (friend of God). William Barclay calls Luke 1:1–4, "well-nigh the best Greek in the New Testament."[1]
- Luke records the first hints of Christian hymnology (1:46–55, 68–79; 2:14, 29–32).
- More pictures have been painted by artists who derive their inspiration from Luke than any other New Testament book.
- Between chapters 9 and 19 there are over 30 sayings, parables, and incidents mentioned nowhere else in Scripture.

The Son of Man . . .

. . . Announced and Appearing

About 90 percent peculiar to Luke

"Jesus the Nazarene, who was a prophet . . . mighty in *deed* . . . and *word* in the sight of God and all the people." (24:19)

. . . Ministering and Serving

. . . Instructing and Submitting

About 60 percent peculiar to Luke

. . . Crucified, Resurrected, and Commissioning

Key Verse	"For the Son of Man has come to seek and to save that which was lost." (19:10)				
	1:1–4	1:5 4:13 4:14	9:50 9:51	19:28 21:38	22:1–24:53
Activity	Unique Introduction	Coming	Seeking		Saving
Location		Bethlehem, Nazareth, and Judea	Galilee	Judea and Perea	Jerusalem
Time		30 years	1 1/2 years	6 mos.	8 days 50 days

1. William Barclay, *The Gospel of Luke*, rev. ed., The Daily Study Bible Series (Philadelphia, Pa.: Westminster Press, 1975), p. 2.

Chapter 1

There Is *Always* Hope

Luke 7:1–17

According to Max Lucado, in his book *When God Whispers Your Name*, the message that popular Christianity teaches is not too different than the message of the classic movie *The Wizard of Oz*.

> The movie ends with Dorothy discovering that her worst nightmare was in reality just a bad dream. That her somewhere-over-the-rainbow home was right where she'd always been. And that it's nice to have friends in high places, but in the end, it's up to you to find your way home.
>
> The moral of *The Wizard of Oz*? Everything you may need, you've already got.
>
> The power you need is really a power you already have. Just look deep enough, long enough, and there's nothing you can't do.
>
> Sound familiar? Sound patriotic? Sound . . . Christian?
>
> For years it did to me. I'm an offspring of sturdy stock. A product of a rugged, blue-collar culture that honored decency, loyalty, hard work and loved Bible verses like, "God helps those who help themselves." (No, it's not in there.) . . .
>
> But, alas, therein lies the problem. As the Teacher said, "No one is good" (Matt. 19:17 NKJV). Nor is anyone always strong; nor is anyone always secure.
>
> Do-it-yourself Christianity is not much encouragement to the done in and the worn out.
>
> Self-sanctification holds little hope for the addict.
>
> "Try a little harder" is little encouragement for the abused.
>
> At some point we need more than good advice;

1

we need help. Somewhere on this journey home we realize that a fifty-fifty proposition is too little. We need more—more than a pudgy wizard who thanks us for coming but tells us the trip was unnecessary. We need help.[1]

We need Jesus.

Two Tragic Scenes of Human Need

In our passage from Luke, Jesus touches the lives of two people whose yellow brick roads have led them into dead-end canyons. Here, no rainbows grace the sky. No good witches float down to fill their hearts with hope. No wizards appear to point out their hidden strengths. They are at the end of their resources.

The Need

The first person lives in Capernaum, where Jesus has recently come (Luke 7:1). He is a Roman centurion—an officer in charge of one hundred soldiers, "the backbone of the Roman army."[2] His slave, "who was highly regarded by him, was sick and about to die" (v. 2).

It could be that the slave had been like a father to him through the years, or if he is younger, like his own brother. The stalwart soldier can't just sit and watch his dear friend die. But what can he do? If you've ever clung to a loved one hanging over death's abyss and felt your fingers slowly losing grip, you know the centurion's awful sense of helplessness.

About twenty-five miles away in the village of Nain, another person stands on death's crumbling ledge. A widow. She has been here before to watch the depths consume her husband. But now she is back, this time with her only son. In horror, she watches him slide over the edge. With him goes her last, tattered vestiges of hope. It is the day of his funeral when she crosses paths with Jesus.

The centurion of Capernaum and the widow of Nain—two people groping for hope in the darkness but finding nothing to hang on to . . . until they meet Jesus.

1. Max Lucado, *When God Whispers Your Name* (Dallas, Tex.: Word Publishing, 1994), pp. 125–126.
2. William Barclay, *The Gospel according to Luke*, rev. ed., The Daily Study Bible Series (Philadelphia, Pa.: Westminster Press, 1975), p. 84.

The Details

Hearing that Jesus is in the area, the centurion decides to risk his reputation by going to a Jew for help. He's a Roman, a soldier in the imperial army, yet before Jesus he becomes a child. Feeling unfit to approach Jesus himself, he formulates a plan:

> And when he heard about Jesus, he sent some Jewish elders asking Him to come and save the life of his slave. And when they had come to Jesus, they earnestly entreated Him, saying, "He is worthy for You to grant this to him; for he loves our nation, and it was he who built us our synagogue." (vv. 3–5)

The elders vouch for their Gentile friend. He is a man of integrity and well-liked by the Jews. More importantly, however, he is a man of faith.

> Now Jesus started on His way with them; and when He was already not far from the house, the centurion sent friends, saying to Him, "Lord, do not trouble Yourself further, for I am not worthy for You to come under my roof; for this reason I did not even consider myself worthy to come to You, but just say the word, and my servant will be healed. For I, too, am a man under authority, with soldiers under me; and I say to this one, 'Go!' and he goes; and to another, 'Come!' and he comes; and to my slave, 'Do this!' and he does it." (vv. 6–8)

Unlike the Pharisees, the centurion doesn't ply Jesus for His credentials. He doesn't even ask to meet Him. Respectfully, he kneels before the divine authority. All Jesus must do is say the word, and it's as good as done.

Now let's switch scenes to Nain where the characters and circumstances differ from those in Capernaum. The widow knows nothing of Jesus; her world is limited to a darkened sphere of grief. Unlike the slave, her loved one has already died. Unlike the centurion, she doesn't approach Jesus with an eloquent request. She's too torn even to pray.

Passing by, Jesus sees the shattered pieces of her life heaped in the coffin and strewn along the funeral route. His heart filled with compassion, He extends a tender touch. "Do not weep," He says

3

gently, as if brushing away her tears (v. 13b).

The contrasts between the widow and the centurion are striking, aren't they? The following chart highlights them for us.

The Centurion	The Widow
The centurion's slave is sick (v. 2).	The widow's son is dead (v. 12).
The centurion makes a request (v. 3).	The widow makes no request (v. 13a).
Jesus and the centurion never meet or communicate directly. Instead, the centurion sends messengers to talk for him (vv. 4–5).	Jesus meets the widow face-to-face, looks into her tear-filled eyes, and gently speaks to her sorrow (v. 13).
The centurion expresses great faith in Christ's authority to heal his slave (vv. 6–8).	Overwhelmed by sorrow, the widow is too distressed even to pray (v. 14a).

The two situations are as different as the characters themselves. In one scene, there is a confident, clear-thinking soldier; in the other, a vulnerable widow, drowning in her turbulent emotions. In one, there is unquestioning faith—"just say the word, and my servant will be healed" (v. 7); in the other, grief as if there is no tomorrow. In one, there is eloquence and protocol; in the other, unbridled pain and enough tears to dissolve the strongest prayers.

These differences illustrate that our Savior doesn't demand that we fit into a set pattern to receive His help. He doesn't restrain His compassion because we fail to meet our "good deeds quota." Or because we don't say the right words. Or because we forget to follow the correct ritual. All that He requires is that we admit our need.

The old adage "God helps those who help themselves" doesn't wash here. Our God is the kind of God who helps the helpless, gives hope to the hopeless, breathes life into the lifeless. His river of compassion never runs dry. It's always overflowing with a cool sip of hope for the parched lips of the suffering.

The Response

The way Jesus extends His help varies in each situation. Notice that in response to the centurion's initial request, Jesus simply starts walking (v. 6a). Jesus could have healed the slave with a word. This being an emergency, why did He wait? Why didn't He say the word then and there?

When it comes to our growth process, the Lord is never in a hurry. We focus on the present need, but God sees the bigger picture. He's more interested in helping us grow through our problems than fixing them for us right away. By waiting, Jesus allows the centurion's budding faith to blossom into maturity. And when it does (vv. 6b–8), Jesus is swift to respond:

> Now when Jesus heard this, He marveled at him, and turned and said to the multitude that was following Him, "I say to you, not even in Israel have I found such great faith." And when those who had been sent returned to the house, they found the slave in good health. (vv. 9–10)

Concerning the widow, Jesus could have simply served up a word of comfort, and that would have been enough. But out of the depths of His mercy, He produces an incredible miracle.

> And He came up and touched the coffin; and the bearers came to a halt. And He said, "Young man, I say to you, arise!" And the dead man sat up, and began to speak. And Jesus gave him back to his mother. And fear gripped them all, and they began glorifying God, saying, "A great prophet has arisen among us!" and, "God has visited His people!" And this report concerning Him went out all over Judea, and in all the surrounding district. (vv. 14–17)

We place our hopes in what we see. When the lungs cease breathing and the heart stops pumping, we say, "That's it. Finished." But Jesus sees beyond the physical to the spiritual. He has the power to resuscitate the dead, to reunite spirit and body. And that is our ultimate hope, isn't it? Not just resuscitation, but resurrection. Some day, the final enemy will be defeated. The dead in Christ will be raised. And Christ will have done what we were helpless to do on our own—bring us home.

When We Are Faced with Serious Needs

Has your heart run dry of hope? What you need is not a better attitude. You need access to the source of all hope—that which Paul says we do not see but eagerly await (Rom. 8:25). Who can understand our helpless state and link us to God?

And in the same way the Spirit also helps our weakness; for we do not know how to pray as we should, but the Spirit Himself intercedes for us with groanings too deep for words; and He who searches the hearts knows what the mind of the Spirit is, because He intercedes for the saints according to the will of God. (vv. 26–27)

The Holy Spirit not only hears our cries, He translates them into petitions that fall in line with God's will. How reassuring it is to know that, through the Spirit, God answers our prayers with what is best for us.

When your yellow brick road dead-ends, remember a couple of things. First, our Lord is not hindered or limited by the things that make us feel helpless . . . so keep waiting. And second, even though we cannot see Him or touch Him, He is hard at work on our behalf . . . so keep praying. With Christ, there is *always* hope.

 Living Insights

The fact that the grieving widow never asked for a miracle is what makes the miracle so incredible. Author Ken Gire explains:

> It is a miracle done without human prompting. Without thought of lessons to be taught to the disciples. Without thought of deity to be demonstrated to the skeptics.
>
> It is a miracle drawn solely from the well of divine compassion. So free the water. So pure the heart from which it is drawn. So tender the hand that cups it and brings it to this bereaved mother's lips.[3]

The great faith of the centurion inspires us, but the widow's silence gives us hope. Jesus cares, even in our weakest moments.

Sometimes we feel our faith turn to sand. Grain by grain, it slowly pours through our theological sieves and out of our hearts. We envy others' centurion-like faith. Secretly, we wonder whether God hears our prayers or sees our suffering or notices our tears.

---

3. Ken Gire, *Incredible Moments with the Savior* (Grand Rapids, Mich.: Zondervan Publishing House, 1990), pp. 43–44.

Surely, Luke included the miracle of the widow's son in his gospel for times like these. "Yes," Luke reassures us, "Jesus hears. He sees. And though we may not have the faith to realize it, He notices our tears and matches them with His own."

If you've sensed your faith wavering lately, don't draw back from the Lord. Let your heartache draw you nearer to the One who cares enough to spare a miracle for a widow in her grief.

 Living Insights

Promises, promises. The TV announcer promises that this gadget is the answer to every busy mother's prayer. The salesperson guarantees that this gizmo will make a "healthier, happier, more tantalizing you." The blue-eyed Casanova vows his undying devotion "'til the stars fall from the sky."

Right.

With promises flying at us from all directions, which ones do we duck and which ones do we hang on to? Whom can we believe?

It wasn't easy for Abraham to believe God's promise. It's hard to image yourself the father of a great nation when you have no children. Yet, as Paul writes, "in hope against hope he believed" (Rom. 4:18). Then, finally, when he was about one hundred years old, his wife had a baby (see vv. 19–21), and the rest is history.

Are you in a situation in which God is asking you to trust Him and keep waiting? Does it sometimes feel like you're hoping against hope? Explain what's happening.

_____

_____

_____

_____

God's promise-keeping record is described in Hebrews 6:13–18. Take a moment to read those verses and jot down some reasons for taking God at His word.

_____

_____

_____

Sometimes we wish we could see God just once, then hoping in Him would be easier. But, as Paul says, "hope that is seen is not hope" (Rom. 8:24). Jesus acknowledged it would be hard: "Blessed are they who did not see, and yet believed" (John 20:29). He's cheering for you to keep on hoping and believing—He and a host of others like Abraham who know it's worth the wait.

> This hope we have as an anchor of the soul, a hope both sure and steadfast. (Heb. 6:19a)

Chapter 2

IN DEFENSE OF A DOUBTER
Luke 7:18–35

Because of Christ, we always have hope. We can bask in the warmth and light of His radiance like the surface of the sea glistens under the sun.

But sometimes a heaviness settles on our souls. Questions about God, like chains of iron, strap themselves around our faith. Doubt starts dragging us under; hope's light dims; and down we go . . .

> descending,
>
> descending,
>
> descending.

We sink into an abyss of uncertainty. Darkness engulfs us. We feel terribly alone.

What causes this plummeting bewilderment? What makes us question the Lord we love? Let's consider a few of the heaviest sources of doubt.

Things That Lead to Times of Doubt

Probably all of us, at one time or another, have felt the weight of at least one of the following three dilemmas.

All of Us, in General

First, *life's inequities offend us.* When hardships lack reason or calamities defy justification, we tend to doubt God's divine purpose in our lives. How can God be in control when evil seems out of control?

Second, *unanswered prayers confuse us.* When we pray for what we know is God's will according to Scripture and nothing happens, we wonder about God's goodness. Does God care about our prayers?

Third, *unfair treatment troubles us.* When we do what's right and suffer for it, we question God's justice. Is God fair?

Questions like these fetter our spirits. We try to go to church, but worship feels forced. Sermon points jangle like prison keys . . . that pass right by our cell. Light conversation only further confines our heavy hearts in isolation.

Does that mean we should be afraid of questions? Shove them out of our minds at their first appearance? No, because sometimes it's in the depths of doubt that we discover God's richest treasures. Instead of making us sinking swimmers or prisoners in a brig, questions make us deep-sea divers, searching for truth. They lead us to a stronger faith. As Tennyson once wrote,

> There lives more faith in honest doubt,
> Believe me, than in half the creeds.[1]

Almost all of Scripture's heroes at one time or another submerged to the briny bottom of doubt's despair. Abraham. Moses. David. Even the foremost voice of faith in the gospels and the subject of our passage, John the Baptizer.

John, Specifically

His angelic birth announcement, his miraculous conception, his father's prophecy, and even his name gave John a sense of mission. He was God's steel-tipped arrow, tempered in the desert and aimed right at the heart of the nation. John was a prophet. And like so many of the prophets, he found himself in mortal combat with despair and its chief envoy, doubt.

A Closer Look at What Transpired

John's first distress signal flared in the form of a question, sent up from the depths of his anguished heart.

Jesus with John's Disciples

> And the disciples of John reported to him about
> all these things [the miracles at Capernaum and Nain].
> And summoning two of his disciples, John sent them
> to the Lord, saying, "Are You the Expected One, or
> do we look for someone else?" (Luke 7:18–19)

Could this be the same man who, just a few months earlier, had flashed his announcement like lightning across a black sky? "Behold, the Lamb of God who takes away the sin of the world!" (John 1:29) Somewhere along the line, his exclamation point had secretly

---

1. Alfred, Lord Tennyson, from "In Memoriam," in *Masterpieces of Religious Verse*, ed. James Dalton Morrison (New York, N.Y.: Harper and Brothers Publishers, 1948), p. 387.

curled into a question mark: "*Are* You the Expected One?"

Having stepped out of the desert of Judea, John is now drowning in an unfamiliar sea of doubt. According to Max Lucado,

> John had never known doubt. Hunger, yes. Loneliness, often. But doubt? Never. Only raw conviction, ruthless pronouncements, and rugged truth. Such was John the Baptist. Conviction as fierce as the desert sun.
>
> Until now. Now the sun is blocked. Now his courage wanes. Now the clouds come. And now, as he faces death, he doesn't raise a fist of victory; he raises only a question. His final act is not a proclamation of courage, but a confession of confusion: "Find out if Jesus is the Son of God or not."
>
> The forerunner of the Messiah is afraid of failure. *Find out if I've told the truth. Find out if I've sent people to the right Messiah. Find out if I've been right or if I've been duped.*[2]

What was the source of John's fear? Although Luke doesn't say exactly, we can follow a few trails to some possible answers.

First, we must remember John's situation. As Luke mentioned back in chapter 3, King Herod had thrown John in prison (see Luke 3:18–20). The bleakness of the dungeon had most likely taken its toll on his spirit. F. B. Meyer writes:

> He was the child of the desert. The winds that swept across the waste were not freer. The boundless spaces of the Infinite had stretched above him, in vaulted immensity, when he slept at night or wrought through the busy days; and as he found himself cribbed, cabined, and confined in the narrow limits of his cell, his spirits sank. . . . Is it hard to understand how . . . the depression of his physical life cast a shadow on his soul?[3]

Second, it could be that John's well-meaning friends slanted

---

2. Max Lucado, *When God Whispers Your Name* (Dallas, Tex.: Word Publishing, 1994), pp. 27–28.

3. F. B. Meyer, *John the Baptist* (reprint, Fort Washington, Pa.: Christian Literature Crusade, 1983), p. 113.

their report, planting doubt in his mind. Meyer supposes some questions about Jesus that may have been drifting through the stale dungeon air:

> Was not all power at His disposal? Did He not wield the sceptre of the house of David? Surely He would not let his faithful follower lie in the despair of that dark dungeon! In that first sermon at Nazareth, of which he had been informed, was it not expressly stated . . . that He would open prison-doors, and proclaim liberty to captives? He would surely then send his angels to open his prison-doors, and lead him forth into the light! But the weeks grew to months, and still no help came. It was inexplicable to John's honest heart, and suggested the fear that he had been mistaken after all.[4]

Third, his disciples' description of Jesus' healings and mercies may have surprised John. According to Meyer, John probably saw the Messiah as

> the Avenger of sin, the Maker of revolution, the dread Judge of all. There was apparently no room in his conception for the gentler, sweeter, tenderer aspects of his Master's nature.[5]

In the fraying fabric of his simple but desperate question, "Are you the Expected One?" John bundles up all his doubts. Then he gives the burdensome package to his messengers, who deliver it just as John asks (7:20).

When Jesus feels the weight of John's struggle, He doesn't stop to lecture. He doesn't rebuke His friend. In fact, He doesn't say anything at first. Mere words cannot lift John's burden. Instead, Jesus lets His actions do the talking.

> At that very time He cured many people of diseases and afflictions and evil spirits; and He granted sight to many who were blind. And He answered and said to them, "Go and report to John what you have seen and heard: the blind receive sight, the lame walk,

4. Meyer, *John the Baptist*, p. 114.

5. Meyer, *John the Baptist*, p. 115.

the lepers are cleansed, and the deaf hear, the dead are raised up, the poor have the gospel preached to them." (vv. 21–22)

Only God's tangible, touchable display of power can penetrate the thick walls of doubt, so Jesus tells the messengers, "You be John's eyes and ears. You tell him you've seen the Messiah—the one who conquers kingdoms not with military might but with the armies of love and mercy."

Then, for John's sake, Jesus adds a beatitude: "Blessed is he who keeps from stumbling over Me" (v. 23). Meyer says, "This is the beatitude of the unoffended, of those who do not stumble over the mystery of God's dealings with their life."[6]

Blessed are the Jobs, who suffer yet stay faithful.

Blessed are the Josephs, who endure unjust treatment yet refuse to live in bitterness.

Blessed are the Hoseas, who continue to walk in obedience even though their spouses leave them.

Blessed are the Pauls, who pray for relief from a thorn in the flesh yet also respond, "His grace is sufficient for me" (see 2 Cor. 12:9).

Blessed are all those who can live with unanswered questions, who can rest in what they see, and who can wait patiently for God to reveal what they can't see.

Jesus with the Multitudes

After John's disciples leave, Jesus takes the opportunity to teach His disciples some important lessons about true greatness.

> And when the messengers of John had left, He began to speak to the multitudes about John, "What did you go out into the wilderness to look at? A reed shaken by the wind? But what did you go out to see? A man dressed in soft clothing? Behold, those who are splendidly clothed and live in luxury are found in royal palaces. But what did you go out to see? A prophet? Yes, I say to you, and one who is more than a prophet. This is the one about whom it is written,
>   'Behold, I send My messenger before Your face,
>   Who will prepare Your way before You.'

6. Meyer, *John the Baptist*, p. 120.

I say to you, among those born of women, there is no one greater than John; yet he who is least in the kingdom of God is greater than he." (Luke 7:24–28)

For those of us whose faith has ever wavered, Jesus' affirmation of John flows over our hearts like a refreshing river over cracked, dried earth. Jesus doesn't condemn us, even when we bring Him our hardest, most desperate doubts.

The people who overheard John's trembling question, however, may not have been so understanding. *Some strong leader John turned out to be,* they may have thought. But Jesus rushed to John's defense: "This man is no reed, blown around by winds of popular opinion. He's no pampered prince, unaccustomed to hardship. He's a prophet and more—the greatest human being who ever lived!"

Like a calming tide, Jesus' opinion of John spreads to those in the crowd who had been his followers. They recognize God's hand on John's life, despite the hardship he is presently enduring.

And when all the people and the tax-gatherers heard this, they acknowledged God's justice, having been baptized with the baptism of John. (v. 29)

The Pharisees and legalists in the crowd, however, stand firm against John . . . and Jesus, for that matter. Jesus' next comments are addressed to them.

Jesus with the Pharisees and Lawyers

But the Pharisees and the lawyers rejected God's purpose for themselves, not having been baptized by John. "To what then shall I compare the men of this generation, and what are they like? They are like children who sit in the market place and call to one another; and they say, 'We played the flute for you, and you did not dance; we sang a dirge, and you did not weep.' For John the Baptist has come eating no bread and drinking no wine; and you say, 'He has a demon!' The Son of Man has come eating and drinking; and you say, 'Behold, a gluttonous man, and a drunkard, a friend of tax-gatherers and sinners!' Yet wisdom is vindicated by all her children." (vv. 30–35)

These same Pharisees who have rejected John are also pushing

Jesus aside. They are impossible to please, like whining children who can't get others to do what they want. They turned up their noses at the bread-and-water truth of John, and now they are making sour faces at the sumptuous delights that Jesus offers. Their self-righteous taste buds find fault in everything set before them.

Wisdom's children, however, accept God's truth hungrily and with gratitude. Tragically, the Pharisees starved while delicious, soul-satisfying food passed them by.

Lessons to Be Learned from Jesus' Example

What spiritual riches might we discover in the depths of our experiences with doubt? From Christ's gracious response to John, the treasure chest is filled with at least three gold medallions of truth.

Medallion one: *Doubting may temporarily disturb us, but it doesn't permanently destroy our relationship with Christ.* The Christian philosopher Blaise Pascal once said,

> We must know where to doubt, where to feel certain,
> where to submit. He who does not do so, under-
> stands not the force of reason.[7]

Doubt leads us past certainty to the point of submission, the very core of our relationship with Christ. It is a narrow passage. Friends may wish to spare us the pain. But we must travel through on our own.

Medallion two: *Blessings rest upon those who can live with earthly inequities, knowing there are heavenly purposes.* The problem is that we don't know what those heavenly purposes are. And that's what makes evils like John getting thrown into prison so hard to understand. Still, Jesus says, "Blessed is he who keeps from stumbling over Me" (v. 23).

Medallion three: *Being childlike is commendable, but being childish is unacceptable.* To doubt is one thing, but to throw Christ's spiritual food on the ground and stomp away mad is another entirely. Don't let lapses in faith hinder you from searching God's Word. Instead, let your questions stimulate your hunger and thirst for righteousness, for then you will be satisfied (see Matt. 5:6).

---

7. Blaise Pascal, as quoted by Daniel Taylor in *The Myth of Certainty* (Grand Rapids, Mich.: Zondervan Publishing House, 1992), p. 95.

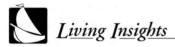

For John, Herod's prison had become a "Doubting Castle." That phrase comes from John Bunyan's classic allegory, *Pilgrim's Progress*. In the story, Christian and Hopeful wander off their path and are captured by the Giant Despair, who throws them into a dungeon in Doubting Castle—

> a nasty, stinking place. There they lay from Wednesday until Saturday night without food or water and without a ray of light or anyone to console them. They were in a pitiful plight, far from friends and acquaintances.[8]

When your faith wavers, does it feel like you're locked in a dark dungeon with Giant Despair glowering at you? Describe what happens in your spirit during times of doubt.

_____

_____

_____

John didn't attempt to handle his doubts alone. He confided in his friends and offered his questions to the Lord. When inequities offend you, unanswered prayers confuse you, or unfair treatment troubles you, where do you go for counsel?

_____

_____

_____

Do you sometimes feel afraid to voice your secret questions? If you're struggling to find a safe place to unburden your heart, ask the Lord to show you to someone you can trust. Jot down any ideas He brings to mind.

_____

---

8. John Bunyan, *Pilgrim's Progress in Today's English*, retold by James H. Thomas (Chicago, Ill.: Moody Press, 1964), p. 114.

You might find a kindred spirit in one or two authors. We recommend James Dobson, *When God Doesn't Make Sense* (Wheaton, Ill.: Tyndale House Publishers, 1993); Daniel Taylor, *The Myth of Certainty: Trusting God, Asking Questions, Taking Risks* (Grand Rapids, Mich.: Zondervan Publishing House, 1992); and Philip Yancey, *Disappointment with God* (Grand Rapids, Mich.: Zondervan Publishing House, 1988).

 Living Insights

There's a difference between seekers like John and scoffers like the Pharisees. The two may ask the same hard questions, but, as Proverbs says, "A scoffer seeks wisdom, and finds none" (14:6). Why? Because scoffers refuse to "go to the wise" for answers (15:12). They have closed their minds. Nothing satisfies them. And every time people try to reach out to them, the scoffers slap their hands.

> He who corrects a scoffer gets dishonor for himself,
> And he who reproves a wicked man gets insults for
>   himself. (9:7)

Seekers, however, ask tough questions with their faces turned upward and their hearts open. Read Proverbs 2:1–7, and note the ways a seeker searches for answers as well as the Lord's response to this kind of openness.

_____

_____

_____

_____

Determine to be a seeker, not a scoffer, the next time questions about your faith arise in your heart.

Chapter 3

JESUS AT HIS BEST

Luke 7:36–50

While families gather for dinner and close their doors for the night, her workday begins. With saffron scarves and lavender veils, dangling earrings and a dab of perfume, she dresses herself for show. Lingering enticingly at her corner, she survives by her looks . . . and looks she'll get. A leer. A scowl. A wink. A sneer. All sorts of looks—except one. Love.

She is a prostitute.

How many times has her heart ached to be wanted for more than one night? To be valued instead of evaluated? To be prized instead of priced? How often has she thought about quitting, only to feel that it's useless. Her scarlet letter will never rub clean.

This day, though, she will meet what she's hardly dared to hope for. She will meet love. She will meet kindness. She will meet Jesus. And He will open the door to her prison of self-condemnation with a key available to us all—a key called acceptance.

The Grace of Acceptance

Acceptance is the fruit people taste when we show them love. It means allowing others to be who they are without disapproving of or losing patience with them. Acceptance is an invitation to freedom. As author Gladys Hunt says:

> It means you are valuable just as you are. It allows you to be the *real* you. You aren't forced into someone else's idea of who you really are. . . .
>
> . . . You feel safe. No one will pronounce judgment on you, even though they don't agree with you. It doesn't mean you will never be corrected or shown to be wrong; it simply means it is safe to be *you* and no one will destroy *you* out of prejudice.[1]

Acceptance can be the most precious gift we give anyone—a family member, a fellow believer, a neighbor. What makes it so

---

1. Gladys M. Hunt, "That's No Generation Gap!" *Eternity*, October 1969, p. 15.

valuable? First, *it allows all judgment to rest with the Lord, not us.* We don't have to assume a role we weren't meant to fill. Paul reminds us,

> Who are you to judge the servant of another? To his own master he stands or falls; and stand he will, for the Lord is able to make him stand. . . . But you, why do you judge your brother? Or you again, why do you regard your brother with contempt? For we shall all stand before the judgment seat of God. (Rom. 14:4, 10)

Second, *it provides each person the freedom to choose.* According to Paul, the choice between two paths in life is often simply a matter of conscience and personal preference:

> One man regards one day above another, another regards every day alike. Let each man be fully convinced in his own mind. (v. 5)

Third, *it helps us focus on essentials, not incidentals.* Usually, when we start judging others, it's because we're preoccupied with insignificant externals. Paul sets our priorities with these words:

> For the kingdom of God is not eating and drinking, but righteousness and peace and joy in the Holy Spirit. (v. 17)

Love calibrates our scales to Christ's standard of measure. We begin to see people as He does. We open our hearts as He opens His. And we freely accept others just as He accepted the self-righteous Pharisee and the broken prostitute.

Jesus: A Model of Love worth Studying

As we enter the story, Jesus' ministry has taken off. He has made many friends and not a few enemies, especially among the jealous Pharisees. So it is interesting that a Pharisee should extend a seemingly friendly gesture and invite Jesus to his house for dinner.

A Pharisee's Invitation to Dinner: Accepted

> Now one of the Pharisees was requesting Him to dine with him. And He entered the Pharisee's house, and reclined at the table. (Luke 7:36)

Now what would this Pharisee, named Simon, want with Jesus?

William Barclay theorizes that he wasn't an admirer, because he neglects good manners when Jesus arrives at his home. Nor is he trying to entrap Him, because he does seem to have some genuine regard for Jesus (he calls Him "Teacher" in verse 40). So he probably "was a collector of celebrities"—inviting Him over out of curiosity.[2]

Whatever his motivation, the Pharisee offers Jesus a social grace, and the Savior graciously accepts. He's willing to show acceptance even to his opposition.

William Barclay gives us a peek inside the Pharisee's house.

> The houses of well-to-do people were built round an open courtyard . . . and there in the warm weather meals were eaten. It was the custom that when a Rabbi [Teacher] was at a meal in such a house, all kinds of people came in—they were quite free to do so—to listen to the pearls of wisdom which fell from his lips. . . .
>
> When a guest entered such a house three things were always done. The host placed his hand on the guest's shoulder and gave him the kiss of peace. That was a mark of respect which was never omitted in the case of a distinguished Rabbi. The roads were only dust tracks, and shoes were merely soles held in place by straps across the foot. So always cool water was poured over the guest's feet to cleanse and comfort them. Either a pinch of sweet-smelling incense was burned or a drop of attar of roses was placed on the guest's head. These things good manners demanded. . . .
>
> In the east the guests did not sit, but reclined, at table. They lay on low couches, resting on the left elbow, leaving the right arm free, with the feet stretched out behind; and during the meal the sandals were taken off.[3]

All the makings of an uneventful, pleasant evening, wouldn't you say?

---

2. William Barclay, *The Gospel of Luke*, rev. ed., The Daily Study Bible Series (Philadelphia, Pa.: Westminster Press, 1975), pp. 94–95.

3. Barclay, *The Gospel of Luke*, p. 94.

A Woman's Act of Devotion: Accepted

Into this refined garden party comes a woman, a prostitute, unclean and out of place. She has taken a risk in coming into a Pharisee's house, but she wants to find Jesus—the great teacher, the friend of sinners she has heard so much about. When her eyes finally rest on Him, the other guests fade in a mist of tears; it suddenly doesn't matter what respectable people think about her. All she sees is Jesus.

Her actions. Luke describes what she does next.

> She brought an alabaster vial of perfume, and standing behind Him at His feet, weeping, she began to wet His feet with her tears, and kept wiping them with the hair of her head, and kissing His feet, and anointing them with the perfume. (vv. 37b–38)

Tender gratitude and wondering love well up from her heart and find release in her sobs. Proper women keep their hair up in public, but she doesn't care. She needs to wipe away the tear streaks on her Savior's feet. As she does, she kisses them and pours out her precious perfume . . . and her adoring heart.

As the sweet fragrance of her sacrifice fills the room, all eyes turn to Jesus. He's neither embarrassed nor upset at her extravagant display of gratitude. He allows her room to express her deep feelings. He accepts her as she is. Simon, on the other hand, starts doing what Pharisees do best—passing judgment.

Simon's reaction. Oftentimes, the most condemning words we hear are the ones we tell ourselves. And the dialogue in Simon's head diagnoses a deadly sin: pride.

> Now when the Pharisee who had invited Him saw this, he said to himself, "If this man were a prophet He would know who and what sort of person this woman is who is touching Him, that she is a sinner." (v. 39)

With a swift pound of his mental gavel, Simon judges both Jesus and the woman. She is a prostitute—why, the whole town knows that. No righteous man would go near her, certainly would not let her touch him. The verdict is clear: Jesus can't be a prophet, much less a holy man.

Jesus' explanation. Jesus knows who the woman is. Indeed, He knows Simon's thoughts as well. He's a prophet and more—the

Son of God who has the power to forgive sins. Aware of Simon's condemnation, He sets him straight with a story.

> "Simon, I have something to say to you." And he replied, "Say it, Teacher." "A certain moneylender had two debtors: one owed five hundred denarii, and the other fifty. When they were unable to repay, he graciously forgave them both. Which of them therefore will love him more?" (vv. 40–42)

Feigning indifference, Simon replied, "I suppose the one whom he forgave more." And with an incisive play on words, Jesus told him, "You have judged correctly" (v. 43).

Then Jesus does something interesting. He shifts His position so that He faces the woman, silently giving her His attention and acceptance. But he continues to address the haughty Pharisee.

> And turning toward the woman, He said to Simon, "Do you see this woman? I entered your house; you gave Me no water for My feet, but she has wet My feet with her tears, and wiped them with her hair. You gave Me no kiss; but she, since the time I came in, has not ceased to kiss My feet. You did not anoint My head with oil, but she anointed My feet with perfume." (vv. 44–46)

A Teacher's Opportunity to Instruct: Accepted

Luke's account closes with Jesus issuing a couple of never-to-be-forgotten words. The first are to Simon:

> "For this reason I say to you, her sins, which are many, have been forgiven, for she loved much; but he who is forgiven little, loves little." (v. 47)

It's not that the Pharisee needs only a "little" forgiveness. Sins of pride and judging are just as damning as sins of promiscuity. The woman, however, was willing to admit the sickness in her heart and the depth of her need. Simon was not. In the end, pride forfeited Simon's forgiveness and dammed up his heart against love.

Jesus addresses the woman next:

> And He said to her, "Your sins have been forgiven." And those who were reclining at the table with Him began to say to themselves, "Who is this man who

even forgives sins?" And He said to the woman, "Your faith has saved you; go in peace." (vv. 48–50)

With these words, Jesus removes her scarlet letter. The burdens of shame and guilt fall away. And she rises a changed, and loved, woman.

Some Principles That Grow Out of This Scene

We can't leave the Pharisee's house without carrying with us a few lasting impressions.

Simon's walled-off courtyard of self-righteousness reminds us that *pride paralyzes us.* It deadens us to our need and numbs our feelings of gratitude toward God.

The sobbing woman's peace shows us that *forgiveness releases us.* We are happiest when we feel forgiven—free of spiritual debt, free of guilt, free of shame.

Jesus' acceptance of the woman tells us that *faith saves us.* Borne on the wings of her love for Christ, she flew to the Pharisee's house to offer her sweet gift. She risked ridicule and disgrace, but she came anyway. Really, that's all faith is. Coming to Jesus. And when we do, we know He'll accept us just as we are.

 Living Insights

Charlotte Elliott had become bedridden while still a young woman in her thirties. Once active and vibrant, she felt useless in her weakened condition and often endured terrible bouts of depression. During one of these dark periods, when her family was out helping her pastor brother raise funds for a Christian school, she lay wondering whether she could ever give anything of value to the Lord. In the midst of her despair, the realization that Jesus found value in her just as she was broke across her mind like a long-awaited sunrise. So relieved, she wrote a song, one that has brought generations to Christ—"Just As I Am."

> Just as I am, tho tossed about
> With many a conflict, many a doubt,
> Fightings and fears within, without,
> O Lamb of God, I come! I come![4]

4. "Just As I Am," third stanza, as quoted by Kenneth W. Osbeck in *101 Hymn Stories* (Grand Rapids, Mich.: Kregel Publications, 1982), p. 146.

Do shortcomings, handicaps, or scars from a painful past fill your life? Do you ever worry that God won't accept you, that He has written you off? Take a moment to write out some of your fears.

_____

_____

_____

Christ opens His arms wide enough to embrace you *and* your burdens. If you've been like one of the guests at the Pharisee's house—listening to Jesus but hesitant to step forward—we encourage you to come to Him, just as you are. We've provided you some space to break your alabaster resistance and pour out the perfume of your life before Him. Express to Him your love, your devotion, your gratitude. Give Him your heart.

_____

_____

_____

_____

_____

_____

_____

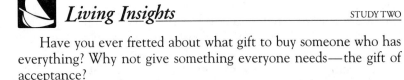 *Living Insights*   STUDY TWO

Have you ever fretted about what gift to buy someone who has everything? Why not give something everyone needs—the gift of acceptance?

Acceptance costs nothing, but it does require sacrifice. It means being willing to love others even though they:

> spill their milk in your lap,
> wear the same fancy dress as you to the wedding,
> drive with one hand on the steering wheel and
>   the other on the radio knob,
> forget the directions,

blow bubbles in their Coke,
arrive fifteen minutes late—all the time,
give advice when you're not asking for it,
hog the bathroom,
change the channels, and
eat the last cookie.

It means forfeiting the right to always be right. It means cutting down our forest of expectations from which others feel they can never escape. It means loving "sinners"—people very much like us.

To whom can you give this gift? Your spouse? Your child? Your in-laws? Boss? Neighbor? Pastor? List two or three names and what you need to do to show them acceptance.

_____

_____

_____

_____

_____

Remember, it's easier to accept others when we realize how much Christ accepts us and forgives us, again and again and again . . .

Chapter 4
UNSEEN YET SIGNIFICANT CONTRIBUTORS
Luke 8:1–3

I n the beginning, God put His hands into the unformed clay of creation and molded a universe. Light beamed into the darkness. The firmament burst forth like fireworks. The seas churned with life. The beasts stretched and yawned in the new dawn. And man took his first breath in Paradise.

"This is good," God sighed with satisfaction after each stage of the work. Toward the end, though, He suddenly stopped. "This is *not* good," He said.

The angels gasped. Creation held its breath. What could be wrong?

> Then the Lord God said, "It is not good for the
> man to be alone; I will make him a helper suitable
> for him." (Gen. 2:18)

The next thing Adam knew, a rib was missing and there stood Eve—the perfect companion. God stepped back with a smile as broad as the blue sky. "Now," He said, brushing off His hands, "this is good. This is very good!"

From the beginning, God designed people to be together. He meant us to live in community, as husband and wife, as families, as friends. Some may try to wave a flag of independence, saying, "I'm my own person. I don't need anybody!" But none of us can function in isolation. No matter how talented or intelligent or capable we are, we need each other.

A Long-Overdue Commendation

According to God's order of things, everyone has a contribution to make for the good of the whole. Just think of the many members of a church who work together. Teachers, technicians, musicians, artists, counselors, craftsmen, administrators . . . the list could go on and on.

To help us function together as one body, the Holy Spirit distributes various spiritual gifts.

> Now there are varieties of gifts, but the same
> Spirit. . . . But to each one is given the manifes-
> tation of the Spirit for the common good. . . .
>
> For even as the body is one and yet has many
> members, and all the members of the body, though
> they are many, are one body, so also is Christ. . . .
> For the body is not one member, but many. (1 Cor.
> 12:4, 7, 12, 14)

Some people question their value because they don't have the
more visible gifts. But Paul responds, "If [we] were all one member,
where would the body be?" (v. 19). In a body, the toes are just as
important as the fingers. And in a church, those who work the
lights are just as important as those who stand in front of them.

To be sure, God notices our unseen contributions. Even a cup
of cold water given in love will bring its divine compensation (see
Matt. 10:42). And those who quietly sow and plant and water in
others' lives "will receive [their] own reward" (1 Cor. 3:8). For

> God is not unjust so as to forget your work and the
> love which you have shown toward His name, in
> having ministered and in still ministering to the
> saints. (Heb. 6:10)

Every act of kindness, every gracious word, every bit of energy
invested in His name God logs in His book to be paid out with
rich dividends in heaven.

A Seldom-Mentioned Observation

It's in the spirit of honoring the unsung heroes of the faith that
Luke includes a special mention of Christ's key supporters at the
beginning of chapter 8.

Ministry on the Move

The chapter opens with Jesus and the disciples on the move.

> And it came about soon afterwards, that He be-
> gan going about from one city and village to another,
> proclaiming and preaching the kingdom of God; and
> the twelve were with Him. (v. 1)

Perhaps no longer accepted in the synagogues, Jesus and the
Twelve had taken to the road full-time to be with the people. The

boats of the fisherman-turned-disciples rocked silently in their moorings; their nets lay in storage. "Closed" signs hung in the windows of the other disciples' businesses. They were on their own now, without home, without income, and perhaps feeling like outcasts as they traveled from village to village.

The disciples must have had their concerns in this new venture. Where would their next meal come from? Or where would they sleep when the nights got cold? What if one of them got sick? What if their clothes wore out or their families back home needed help?

It's easy to forget about the everyday needs Jesus and His disciples had. Manna didn't appear on the ground for their breakfast every morning. How did God provide?

People behind the Scenes

Luke tells us the answer in the next two verses. Also traveling with the team were

> some women who had been healed of evil spirits and sicknesses: Mary who was called Magdalene, from whom seven demons had gone out, and Joanna the wife of Chuza, Herod's steward, and Susanna, and many others who were contributing to their support out of their private means. (vv. 2–3)

Did you know that Jesus traveled with more than just His disciples? A whole team of sponsors, like these women, took care of their practical needs: buying food, supplying clothing, making special arrangements. Why would they go to so much trouble? Because Jesus had changed their lives. His power had embraced them, delivered them of demon possession or sickness, and given them a second chance. Gratitude flowed out of their hearts in a steady stream of generosity and devotion.

Let's get to know these benefactors better.

First is "Mary who was called Magdalene"—that is, she was from the town of Magdala, located on the western shore of the Sea of Galilee. Once possessed by seven demons, she found release in Jesus and peace for her tortured soul. In loving response, she would cling to her Savior all the way to the foot of the cross and beyond—to His burial and His empty tomb (see John 19:25; Mark 15:47; 16:1; John 20:11–18).

Second is Joanna. Her husband was Chuza, who, according to William Barclay, was "the official who looked after the king's financial interests. . . . There could be no more trusted and important official."[1] Barclay adds an interesting observation:

> It is an amazing thing to find Mary Magdalene, with the dark past, and Joanna, the lady of the court, in the one company.[2]

Mary and Joanna—two women from different worlds joining hands in their common devotion to Christ. They would even be at the tomb together, bowing before the two dazzling angels who would announce that Christ had risen (Luke 24:1–10).

The third woman is Susanna. This is the only place in all of Scripture that Susanna is mentioned, and Luke chooses not to tell us much about her, except that, along with the rest, she also was "contributing to their support" (8:3b).

That phrase is translated from the Greek verb *diakoneō*, from which we get our word *deacon*. It means "to minister, serve, wait upon . . . to do one a service, care for one's needs."[3] The imperfect tense suggests continuous action. These women were continually caring for the everyday needs of Jesus and the disciples, freeing them up so they could proclaim the gospel.

Luke also says that they served out of "their private means." They made the personal sacrifices necessary to keep the ministry rolling. What a debt we owe these women and the many other *diakonos* who gave their all to make Christ's ministry possible.

Four Rarely Remembered Examples

Many others have contributed to the needs of Christ and His church throughout history, and they, too, can serve as models of generosity for us.

A Man from Cyprus

It's beautiful to see how the gracious attitude of Christ's supporters spilled over, like a river rushing toward a breathtaking waterfall, into the young church in Jerusalem.

---

1. William Barclay, *The Gospel of Luke*, rev. ed., The Daily Study Bible Series (Philadelphia, Pa.: Westminster Press, 1975), p. 96.

2. Barclay, *The Gospel of Luke*, pp. 96–97.

3. G. Abbott-Smith, *A Manual Lexicon of the Greek New Testament*, 3d ed. (Edinburgh, Scotland: T. and T. Clark, 1937), p. 107.

And the congregation of those who believed were of one heart and soul; and not one of them claimed that anything belonging to him was his own; but all things were common property to them. And with great power the apostles were giving witness to the resurrection of the Lord Jesus, and abundant grace was upon them all. For there was not a needy person among them, for all who were owners of land or houses would sell them and bring the proceeds of the sales, and lay them at the apostles' feet; and they would be distributed to each, as any had need. (Acts 4:32–35)

Among these unselfish souls was one particularly gracious man.

Joseph, a Levite of Cyprian birth, who was also called Barnabas by the apostles (which translated means, Son of Encouragement), and who owned a tract of land, sold it and brought the money and laid it at the apostles' feet. (vv. 36–37)

He saw the need in the church. He took a look at his own resources. And, in a beautiful gesture of grace, he spontaneously gave.

The Churches of Macedonia

Over in Macedonia, there lived whole congregations of Barnabases! These generous believers, however, had none of his assets.

Now, brethren, we wish to make known to you the grace of God which has been given in the churches of Macedonia, that in a great ordeal of affliction their abundance of joy and their deep poverty overflowed in the wealth of their liberality. For I testify that according to their ability, and beyond their ability they gave of their own accord, begging us with much entreaty for the favor of participation in the support of the saints. (2 Cor. 8:1–4)

Their giving surprised even Paul—it was "not as we had expected" (v. 5a). What's the secret of such overflowing liberality? Paul says, "They first gave themselves to the Lord" (v. 5b). By giving our hearts to the Lord who gave His life for us, we prepare a seedbed where generosity can grow.

The Saints at Philippi

Some ordinary saints supported Paul in Philippi when no one else would. In his letter to the Philippians, the apostle acknowledged that

> no church shared with me in the matter of giving
> and receiving but you alone. (Phil. 4:15b)

They gave to Paul regularly—"you sent a gift more than once for my needs" (v. 16). Their offerings were "a fragrant aroma, an acceptable sacrifice, well-pleasing to God" (v. 18). Paul was glad about their generosity, not for his sake, but for theirs. They were the ones who would someday receive the Lord's reward. He said, "I seek for the profit which increases to your account" (v. 17).

Instruction on Crete

One of Paul's apprentices, Titus, who ministered on the island of Crete, received this advice from the aging apostle:

> And let our people also learn to engage in good
> deeds to meet pressing needs, that they may not be
> unfruitful. (Titus 3:14)

For fear of abuse, some Christian leaders hesitate to talk about the legitimate needs of a ministry. But in order to experience the joy of giving, Christians must know the facts. Certainly, it is wrong to manipulate people into giving, but that doesn't mean we should shy away from making people aware of ministry opportunities.

This verse also reminds us that, besides financial giving, donating time and talents are ways to meet others' needs.

Three Much-Needed Reminders

The examples of the women who supported Jesus, the early Christians in Jerusalem, the Macedonian believers, the Philippian saints, and the Christians at Crete all add up to this bottom-line principle: *Everyone is important in the Lord's work.*

The church is a body in which every individual member is essential. Have you been giving of yourself to meet the needs of others? If you'd like to contribute more, here are a few reminders to help you follow the examples of the men and women we've just met.

First, *since God owns it all, His work deserves top priority when it comes to how we spend our resources.* It's been said that if you want to know what your priorities are, look at the ledger in your checkbook—and we might add, look at the pages of your calendar. Do these two diaries reveal a generous spirit? If you've given your heart first to the Lord as the Macedonian believers did, the evidence will be unmistakable.

Second, *consistent, generous giving from a ministry calls for consistent, generous giving from the recipients.* The women responded to Jesus' overflowing ministry in their lives with contributions "out of their private means." The various ministries the Lord uses to meet our needs are the ministries that deserve our greatest support.

Third, *releasing our money to meet pressing needs outside our own is a learned trait.* The more we give, the more comfortable we feel giving. The more comfortable we feel, the more joy we experience. The more joy we experience, the more we give. Generosity can be habit forming!

 Living Insights STUDY ONE

Like a mighty river, God's grace flows into our lives to flow out again. "Freely you received, freely give," Jesus said (Matt. 10:8b). God intends us to be open channels of His benefits.

Sometimes, however, we resemble levees, holding back God's strong current of blessings for ourselves. We do this for a variety of reasons. Our spirits may be dry, and we need time to replenish our reservoir. We may not know how or what to give. Or maybe we're afraid. If we see our gift as small or weak, we may fear being made to feel inferior. Or we're afraid that if we give away what God has given us, our needs or desires will go unmet.

Take a moment to evaluate your giving. To what degree do God's resources—possessions, money, time, talents, spiritual blessings—stream in and out of your life? Do they flow freely? Do they get hung up along the way? Are they blocked entirely?

_____

_____

If you resemble a levee more than an open channel, why is that so?

_____

_____

What would remove some of your obstructions to giving?

_____

_____

_____

What God-given benefit can you share with someone this week? If you're unsure what to do, who can help you channel your resources?

_____

_____

 Living Insights

Setting your destination is vital to any journey, whether it be a family vacation or a plan for giving. You may have a clear grasp of your resources, your desire to give may be revved up and ready to go, but where are you going? What is your long-term goal?

Ron Blue defines *stewardship* as "the use of God-given resources for the accomplishment of God-given goals."[4] Besides tithing to your local church, have you thought of funneling certain funds toward specific projects or ministries? Here are a few:

- Support one missionary family throughout their career

- Help one young person per year go to summer camp

- Establish a safe house for abused women

- Set up a scholarship fund for students going into the ministry

- Give to a relief organization that cares for needy children

The list could go on for pages. Won't you ask the Lord what goal He might have for your giving? How exciting it would be to see this goal accomplished through your years of generosity!

---

4. Ron Blue, *Master Your Money*, revised and updated (Nashville, Tenn.: Thomas Nelson Publishers, 1991), p. 23.

Chapter 5

WHERE ARE YOU
IN THIS PICTURE?

Luke 8:4–15

The word was out: Jesus was coming! *Jesus*—the people's Rabbi, the Man with heaven in His touch, the Teacher who could beat the Pharisees at their own game. "He's someone to see," went the local buzz. "Close the shop. Pack a blanket. Bring the baby. Let's go see Jesus!"

Crowds gathered wherever Jesus went. It was as if the countryside had tipped up, and rivers of people were streaming to Him from every corner of Palestine. Any minister would have been thrilled with such a flood of people—and after only a few months of preaching too. Jesus' ministry was a booming success.

Or was it?

By today's bigger-is-better standard, which measures churches by their size and their pastor's drawing power, Jesus had reached the top. It was time to consider contracts, booking agents, and marketing strategies. However, as Jesus scanned the crowds pooling around Him, He was thinking more about hearts than numbers. The larger the crowds, the more He wondered whether these people really understood His message. According to commentator William Arndt,

> With His divine insight He perceived that much of
> what on the surface appeared as genuine devotion
> was in reality nothing but the froth and foam of idle
> curiosity or of sentimental nationalism or of an in-
> tense desire to find material help in the struggle for
> existence.[1]

From Jesus' point of view, it was time to purify, not magnify, the crowd . . . time to separate the serious thinker from the shallow

---

Sections of this chapter are adapted from "An Analysis of a Crop Failure," from the study guide *Growing Up in God's Family*, coauthored by Bryce Klabunde, from the Bible-teaching ministry of Charles R. Swindoll (Anaheim, Calif.: Insight for Living, 1994), pp. 1–6.

1. William F. Arndt, *The Gospel according to St. Luke* (Saint Louis, Mo.: Concordia Publishing House, 1956), p. 226.

observer, to sift the casual onlooker from the devoted disciple. And the best teaching tool for that purpose was the parable.

A Few Comments on Parables

The word *parable* in Greek—from *para*, "alongside," and *ballō*, "to throw"—literally means "to place something alongside." A parable, then,

> is a story in which the teller uses an understood truth about everyday life to teach something that is unknown, placing the familiar alongside the unfamiliar to illustrate one major truth.[2]

Though a familiar illustration helps ground an unfamiliar truth, it still takes discernment from the Holy Spirit, who "searches all things, even the depths of God" (1 Cor. 2:10), to understand the deeper meaning. People who resist the things of the Spirit cannot understand the truth; it is "foolishness" to them (v. 14).[3]

As a result, Christ knew the uncommitted spectators in the crowd would get hung up on His parable, as if caught in a sieve, while the devoted disciples would filter through to discover the heavenly treasure.

The Parable of the Sower and the Seed

Jesus' parable in our passage includes three common elements: a sower, seed, and various types of soil.

The Parable Set Forth

> And when a great multitude were coming together, and those from the various cities were journeying to Him, He spoke by way of a parable: "The sower went out to sow his seed; and as he sowed, some fell beside the road; and it was trampled under foot, and the birds of the air ate it up. And other seed fell on rocky soil, and as soon as it grew up, it withered away, because it had no moisture. And

2. From the study guide *Issues and Answers in Jesus' Day*, coauthored by Ken Gire, from the Bible-teaching ministry of Charles R. Swindoll (Fullerton, Calif.: Insight for Living, 1990), p. 123.

3. The Greek root word for *foolishness* is *mōros*, from which we get our word *moron*. Spiritual things appear moronic to the unbeliever.

other seed fell among the thorns; and the thorns
grew up with it, and choked it out. And other seed
fell into the good soil, and grew up, and produced
a crop a hundred times as great." As He said these
things, He would call out, "He who has ears to hear,
let him hear." (Luke 8:4–8)

The first seed fell "beside the road" on the *hard soil,* where the
farmer and his beast walked between the rows of plants. Because
this soil was trodden on so often, it was packed as solid as asphalt.
The seed, scattered across this impenetrable surface, had no chance
to germinate. Instead, it became fast food for passing birds.

Other seed fell on *rocky soil,* which refers not to stones mixed
in with the soil but to a thin "skin of earth over a shelf of limestone
rock."[4] Without enough depth and nourishment to take root in
such soil, the sprouts would wither under the sun's heat almost as
quickly as they had sprung up.

Seed also landed in *thorny soil.* Rather than go to the trouble
of pulling the thorny and thistly weeds out by the root, Palestinian
farmers of that day often just cut or burned off the weed tops. The
soil may have looked ready for seed, but

below the surface the roots were still there; and in
due time the weeds revived in all their strength.
They grew with such rapidity and such virulence
that they choked the life out of the seed.[5]

Finally, some seed fell into *good ground.* This soil was carefully
cleared, prepared, tilled, and made ready for planting. So the seed
took root in a nutrient-rich bed that nourished it until it produced
a bumper crop.

So much for our farming lesson! Now, what was the spiritual
jewel in Jesus' story? The disciples were eager to find out.

The Disciples' Questioning

And His disciples began questioning Him as to
what this parable might be. And He said, "To you
it has been granted to know the mysteries of the

---

4. William Barclay, *The Gospel of Mark,* rev. ed., The Daily Study Bible Series (Philadelphia,
Pa.: Westminster Press, 1975), p. 95.

5. Barclay, *The Gospel of Mark,* p. 96.

kingdom of God, but to the rest it is in parables, in
order that seeing they may not see, and hearing they
may not understand." (vv. 9–10)

Simply seeing miracles and hearing teaching doesn't get people
into Jesus' kingdom any more than hearing about good food gives
us a healthy body. We must first eat the food to receive its benefit.
Similarly, we must believe in Jesus to see the truth in His teaching.
Many of the people in Jesus' day saw but didn't see, heard but didn't
hear, because they were unwilling to accept Him first. The disciples,
though, were willing, so Jesus unveiled to them the wealth in His words.

The Parable Interpreted

Jesus begins by explaining that "the seed is the word of God"
(v. 11). The sower, then, would be any messenger who spreads the
principles of God's Word. And the soils symbolize the conditions
of the human heart. It's in the "soils" that we dig up the treasure
in this parable.

The hard heart. The hard soil beside the road represents people
with unresponsive hearts. Jesus says,

"And those beside the road are those who have
heard; then the devil comes and takes away the word
from their heart, so that they may not believe and
be saved." (v. 12)

Like grains of rice on concrete, God's Word only rests on top
of these people's hearts. Nothing the messenger says penetrates the
surface and convinces them of their need for a life-changing, personal relationship with God. They may attend church or hang
around Christians, but because they are hardened to the truth, the
Adversary easily picks off whatever morsels of the gospel land in
their minds. As a result, they remain unrepentant and unsaved.

The shallow heart. The thin, rocky soil represents people with
superficial, impulsive hearts. Jesus continues,

"And those on the rocky soil are those who, when
they hear, receive the word with joy; and these have
no firm root; they believe for a while, and in time
of temptation fall away." (v. 13)

Interestingly, the word *firm* was added to the text (indicated by
italics in the New American Standard Bible); it was not part of the

original phrase and really should not be present now. What Jesus is saying is that the seed of living truth has only been superficially accepted, received with an impulsive joy; but when temptation comes, these people simply fall away because they have no root of faith. They also remain unsaved.

The busy, crowded heart. Jesus explains the thorny soil with its choking weeds as

> "the ones who have heard, and as they go on their way they are choked with worries and riches and pleasures of this life, and bring no fruit to maturity." (v. 14; see also Mark 4:18–19)

These people receive Christ into hearts that become crammed to capacity with anxieties over the political scene, the crime rate, the economy, social obligations, family issues—anything they can worry about. Elbowing in next to these is the drive to get ahead and raise their standard of living; unmasked, it's called materialism. Also jockeying for attention are hobbies and interests that sometimes become obsessions. What can be heard above this din? God's Word can't, and our lives can't be fruitful without it.

The productive, strong heart. The final soil condition represents productive hearts, or Christians who hear, receive, and respond to the seed planted within them. They are the ones

> "who have heard the word in an honest and good heart, and hold it fast, and bear fruit with perseverance." (Luke 8:15)

Notice the three characteristics of "fertile soil" folks. First, they hear with "an honest and good heart." They're open to the truth about themselves. And if they see sin in their lives, they're willing to admit it and change. Second, they hold fast to the Word. Scripture enters their brains and stays there long enough to soak into their will, down to the deepest parts of their being. As a result, third, they "bear fruit with perseverance." Out of their will blossoms an obedience that flowers throughout life, not just for a season.

The main principle of Jesus' parable, then, is this:

The harvest depends on the heart.

It's so simple, we often miss it. Fruitfulness in Christ's kingdom doesn't depend on our talents or abilities. What matters is the condition of our hearts.

Finding Yourself in This Word Picture

What's your heart condition? Are you open? Teachable? Imperfect, to be sure, but honest? Then your heart is fertile ground for God's Word.

Perhaps, though, the worries of life have preoccupied you. A lack of contentment has strangled your peace. Striving for riches and pleasure, you've lost sight of Christ. Your heart has become thorny ground.

Maybe your interest in Christ sprang up quickly but withered in the heat of temptation. Looking back now, you realize that you only wanted to appear Christian rather than commit yourself completely. Your heart is rocky soil.

Or maybe your heart is hard. You have no intention of getting serious about spiritual things.

Which soil represents your heart? While you're thinking, remember this: Jesus is coming . . . but not in the same way as His first visit. This time, He'll put His mighty sickle to the fields and reap the harvest. Then it will be too late for cultivating soil. Prepare your heart now, so when He comes, your life will deliver up a fruitful harvest for eternity.

 Living Insights STUDY ONE

As a novice gardener, one of my first jobs was weeding. I recall the crew leader slapping a hoe in my hands, pointing me toward a planter bursting with scraggly intruders, and wishing me luck. Hoping to make a good impression, I attacked the beasts with a fury that was meant to send a signal of doom to weeds everywhere.

In my impassioned hacking, however, I overlooked one fact—which the boss quickly pointed out to me. Lost in the tangle were some plants worth saving. There were flowers in this flowerbed. Sadly, I couldn't tell a milkweed from a marigold. So he showed me how to tell the difference. From then on, I hoed more carefully, cutting down the invaders while leaving the seedlings that would someday produce beautiful flowers.

Hoeing the weedy desires in our hearts requires similar care. It takes a gardener's eye to spot the difference between a pastime and a preoccupation. Between a diversion and an obsession. Between refreshing entertainment and overgrown greed.

Can you tell when your hobby is developing tendrils and taking over your heart? Some choking signs may appear in the amount of money or time you spend, the relationships you sacrifice, or the spiritual exercise you neglect. Review the state of your planter. Ask the Master Gardener to separate the weeds from the flowers in your heart (see Ps. 139:23–24).

What are some of your pastimes that are healthy and worth cultivating? Write them down so you can plainly see not to hoe them.

Is God showing you some "thorny" preoccupations? What are they?

You can tell these are true weeds by testing certain areas. First, how are they affecting your attitude?

Next, your relationships with others?

How about your relationship with God?

Jesus said that a heart crowded with the "worries and riches and pleasures of this life [will] bring no fruit to maturity" (Luke 8:14b). Do you need to do some weeding in your life? What needs to come out?

Spiritual weeding is not just for novice Christians. Ask God for the skill and patience you'll need so you don't mistakenly pull up some healthy flowers along the way.

 Living Insights

Under ideal conditions, plants can sprout in the rockiest of soils. A barren hillside can grow a lush carpet of grasses—when the rainfall is just right and the weather is temperate. Such is the spiritual climate in these early days of Jesus' ministry. Disciples, like wildflowers, are springing up everywhere.

But summer will come. The religious leaders will bear down on Him with sweltering intensity. And Jesus' uncompromising response and searing words will raise the temperature that much more. Even now, hot winds of persecution are swirling across the horizon.

Needless to say, the heat will wither the rootless disciples. The hillside now flourishing with eager onlookers will be barren once more.

Perhaps you first heard about Christ when the spiritual conditions were just right. At a camp maybe. Or a crusade or conference. At the time, your heart received the Word with joy. But, later, you felt your faith wither in the summer heat of life's difficulties. Maybe reading this study guide is your attempt to recover what you once had but somehow lost.

In the solitude of this moment, we invite you to make the commitment to Christ you were unable to make before. Throw out all your plan-B options. Trust Him with everything. Jesus said,

> "I am the resurrection and the life; he who believes
> in Me shall live even if he dies, and everyone who
> lives and believes in Me shall never die. Do you
> believe this?" (John 11:25–26)

That's the question you must answer. "Do you believe this?"

Chapter 6

HIDDEN SECRETS, FAMILY STRUGGLES, STORMY SEAS

Luke 8:16–25

J esus is not one to stick a Band-Aid on a wound and call it healed. Gently, He probes the hurt until He finds the source of the pain. "This will sting a little," He warns as He reaches in and tugs at the problem until it is removed.

He's right. It does sting. At the moment, we'd rather have a Band-Aid and a sucker. But later, as the wound heals, we thank Him for His careful attention to the deeper need.

Three Stressful Scenes . . . and How to Cope

In the verses we're about to read, Jesus is probing three sensitive spots in our lives: our hidden secrets, our family struggles, and our difficult circumstances. In each of these areas, He'll recommend a treatment that penetrates below the surface to the heart of the matter.

Personal: When Secrets Stay Hidden

Jesus addresses the first and most personal of the three areas, our hidden secrets, with a far-reaching concept summed up in the word *light*.

> "Now no one after lighting a lamp covers it over
> with a container, or puts it under a bed; but he puts
> it on a lampstand, in order that those who come in
> may see the light." (Luke 8:16)

When we become Christians, a light turns on inside us that is difficult to hide. It's the light of Christ's new life, and Jesus says that covering it up would be as nonsensical as lighting a lamp and clapping a bucket over it. Light must shine forth, searching and dispelling the darkness. That's what makes it so wonderful . . . and so unsettling. Jesus, the Light of life, goes on to say,

> "Nothing is hidden that shall not become evident,
> nor anything secret that shall not be known and
> come to light." (v. 17)

Paul concurs: "All things become visible when they are exposed by the light" (Eph. 5:13). *All* things. Even the things we would just as soon keep hidden.

Although most of the doors in our lives stand open, some of them we lock from the inside. They lead to secret passages of past pain . . . inadequacies . . . private addictions. At the entrance to these hidden chambers, we hang No Trespassing signs, warning intruders to keep away.

Why do we zealously guard parts of our lives from the light? To find the answer, we must travel back to the beginning of time, to the moment Adam and Eve sinned. As they bit into the sweet forbidden fruit, bitter consequences dominoed one after the other:

> Then the eyes of both of them were opened, and they knew that they were naked; and they sewed fig leaves together and made themselves loin coverings.
>
> And they heard the sound of the Lord God walking in the garden in the cool of the day, and the man and his wife hid themselves from the presence of the Lord God among the trees of the garden. (Gen. 3:7–8)

Hiding from God. Silly, isn't it? The Lord played along, though—"Where are you?" (v. 9). That's what He said, but the pained tone in His voice asked, "Why are you hiding from Me?" Adam answered,

> "I heard the sound of Thee in the garden, and I was afraid because I was naked; so I hid myself." (v. 10)

"I was afraid"—that's why we hide too. We're afraid that if God or others see the naked truth about us, they will reject us. Just the thought of a searchlight exposing us sends shivers of shame up our spines.

So we become self-conscious. We brush rouge on our cheeks to cover the stains of tears shed in secret. We adjust our stride to appear confident and in control, even though we're stumbling inside.

And we think that nobody sees the truth.

But Jesus says, "Nothing is hidden . . . nor anything secret." Remember Achan's story in the Book of Joshua? He thought he could conceal contraband treasures under his tent. But the Lord brought him before "all Israel," where he could no longer hide his sin (Josh. 7:16–26). And Moses? He was sure no one would find out that he had killed the Egyptian and hidden his body in the sand. But the next thing he knew, it was common knowledge with the Hebrews, and Pharaoh tried to kill him for it (Exod. 2:11–15).

Are you hiding any shameful secrets in the sand? Freedom from guilt and release from stress will elude you until you bring everything into the light.

Trusted friends or counselors can help us through the labyrinth of secret trails in our hearts, but it takes time. Transparent living doesn't happen overnight. It's a part of the growing process called sanctification. Jesus says that, as we give Him our secrets, He'll be there to shine more and more of His healing light into the recesses of our lives until the day we behold the fullness of His glory. All the doors will be open then, and there will be nothing left but light.

Until that magnificent moment, Jesus says,

> "Take care how you listen; for whoever has, to him shall more be given; and whoever does not have, even what he thinks he has shall be taken away from him." (Luke 8:18)

The more we think we have it together, the less open we are to the strength and courage Christ gives us to face the hard issues. But as we knock down the walls of pride and listen to Him with fertile hearts—remember the parable of the soils—Jesus will keep on giving us what we need to grow.

Relational: When Family Remains Distant

Jesus directs His attention to a second area: our families. Here the key concept is *truth*. In the following verses, Jesus relates with His own family in a way that reveals some insights into this most sensitive side of our lives.

> And His mother and brothers came to Him, and they were unable to get to Him because of the crowd. And it was reported to Him, "Your mother and Your brothers are standing outside, wishing to see You." But He answered and said to them, "My mother and My brothers are these who hear the word of God and do it." (vv. 19–21)

Does it strike you as odd that Jesus had a closer relationship with His followers than with His mother and brothers?[1] Mark says

1. The fact that Jesus had brothers and sisters (see Matt. 13:55–56) contradicts the doctrine of Mary's perpetual virginity—the idea that she remained a virgin for the rest of her life.

44

in his gospel that Jesus' family did not believe His messianic claims. On one occasion,

> they went out to take custody of Him; for they were saying, "He has lost His senses." (Mark 3:21)

Little wonder that Jesus distanced Himself from them! They didn't understand or accept Him. His disciples, on the other hand, grasped the truth about Him and His teaching—they were on the same wavelength.

Often, when we are the only Christians in our families, we experience that same alienation with our unsaved relatives; Christ's truth in our lives tends to loosen our family ties. The love is present, but the unity is not. Our paths have changed directions, and we don't view life the same way anymore.

This feeling of separation, even isolation, is part of the "sword" that Jesus said He would bring (see Matt. 10:34–37). He calls His followers to love Him above all others, even mother and father. Unsaved or less mature family members will not understand this commitment and may ridicule us for it. Persecution from anyone is painful, but suffering at the hands of our own loved ones has to be the heaviest of crosses to bear.

It is a cross Christ has borne, though, and one He has overcome. And the intimacy we need is now found with fellow believers in Him.

Circumstantial: When Storms Appear Threatening

From the secrets in our hearts to the struggles in our families, Jesus widens His interest in us to the storms we endure. Concerning this area, He applies the vital principle of *faith*.

> Now it came about on one of those days, that He and His disciples got into a boat, and He said to them, "Let us go over to the other side of the lake." And they launched out. But as they were sailing along He fell asleep. (Luke 8:22–23a)

Resting in the competent hands of the fishermen who guided the rudder and trimmed the sails, Jesus fell asleep to the gentle rocking of the waves. However, it wasn't long before a sudden and fierce gale swept across the cliffs that guarded the Sea of Galilee and descended on the lake, so that: "they began to be swamped and to be in danger" (v. 23b).

The wind whipped the lulling waves into surging walls of water, crashing over the bow and filling the boat. Frantically, the seamen bailed; but for every bucket of water they threw overboard, the sea tossed back twenty more.

Oblivious to the upheaval, Jesus slept on, resting now in the cupped hands of His Father. Soaked and shivering, the men at the oars strained to keep her headed into the wind, but the heavy vessel insisted on sloshing and listing to one side. Any moment she would kneel to the commanding sea.

In a panic, the disciples woke up Jesus, yelling against the storm,

> "Master, Master, we are perishing!" And being aroused, He rebuked the wind and the surging waves, and they stopped, and it became calm. (v. 24)

Immediately, the angry thunderclouds unclenched their fists, and the monstrous waves retreated into the depths. Dazed, the disciples slowly released their grip on the sides of the boat, only for a new fear to grip them as they gazed at the Man who could change the weather with just a word. Rebuking the winds of doubt still surging in their souls, Jesus said:

> "Where is your faith?" And they were fearful and amazed, saying to one another, "Who then is this, that He commands even the winds and the water, and they obey Him?" (v. 25)

We know the answer to the disciples' question: Jesus is the Son of God, the Ruler of Nature. Jesus' question is more difficult. Where is our faith during our storms of life? Is it in circumstances? In people? In ourselves? If so, we're bound to be disappointed. Jesus longs for us to put our trust in Him—the One who can take us through the storm. Not around, not over, but *through* (see Isa. 43:2).

So weatherproof your faith. Build up your courage. Set your sights across the stormy sea. There's more to life than motoring in a protected harbor. With Christ fixing your course; you can afford to take some risks. You can experience the thrill of the open sea.

In Light of Today's Struggles, Remember . . .

Light. Truth. Faith. Three penetrating concepts from Jesus' life and ministry. What do they have to say to us today?

First, *light will keep you from hiding, so let it in*. To explore the secrets in your life, you may need the help of a pastor, counselor, or friend, but stay at it. Get the secrets out in the open. Let Christ's light shine into every corner of your life.

Second, *truth will keep you from running, so let it out.* You may have to initiate a very honest talk with some family members. Don't be afraid to say what Christ means to you. With all the tact and sincerity you can muster, tell the truth.

Third, *faith will keep you from fearing, so let it go.* Fears, like anchors, stop us dead in the water. We fear what people will say. We fear unknown circumstances. We fear failure. But by trusting Christ, the Ruler of the wind and the waves, we can release our fears and start moving forward again.

 Living Insights

How intimate is the printed page! By reading, you invite the writer—a stranger—to talk with you on a crowded bus when you don't feel like talking to anyone else. Or take the seat next to you at the kitchen table during a rare moment of quiet. Or sit on the edge of the bed with you before you reach over and turn out the light.

Knowing this is a privilege and holding it gingerly, I want to ask you a question that perhaps only a writer can ask. How are things going in your private life?

Really. How are you doing?

You may be able to answer with David's confident words to the Lord:

> Though you probe my heart and examine me at
> night,
> though you test me, you will find nothing;
> I have resolved that my mouth will not sin.
> (Ps. 17:3 NIV)

Or you may quake at the thought of standing naked before the Lord's glaring light. David probably would have too, if he hadn't continually invited the Lord to search him, to try him, to know his "anxious thoughts" (Ps. 139:23). Yes, this is the same David who had a secret affair with Bathsheba. Yet he earnestly prayed that God would create in him a "clean heart" and renew a "steadfast spirit" within him (51:10). And the Lord did.

The Lord can do the same for you too. On the altar of this moment, pour out your secrets before Him—the silent grudges, the hidden deeds, the private fears. Invite His light to come like a purifying fire and consume the clutter of your life.

The French have a saying: "There is no pillow so soft as a clear conscience."[2] Let's make a pact together that we're not going to lose sleep fretting that someone might uncover some secret we've been hiding. We're going to keep our consciences clear and clean.

OK? It's a deal!

 ## *Living Insights* STUDY TWO

Our families give us more than just a name and a home to go to for the holidays. They give us our flavor. When God made us, He took little tastes of each family member and formed them into one person. You may have your uncle Henry's sense of humor, your Nana's blue eyes, or your mom's love for music. You are your family.

That's why feeling distant from them because of your faith in Christ tears at your soul. You are truly denying yourself.

What comfort does it bring you knowing that Christ separated from His family?

_____

_____

_____

_____

Read Jesus' special promise to those who forsake family for His sake in Matthew 19:29. When is this assurance most meaningful for you?

_____

_____

_____

_____

2. As quoted by Bob Phillips in *Phillips' Book of Great Thoughts and Funny Sayings* (Wheaton, Ill.: Tyndale House Publishers, 1993), p. 74.

Pamela Reeve, in her little book *Faith Is . . .*, says,

Faith is . . .
. . . Engaging in the deepest joy
of heaven
knowing His unfathomable love
for me
as I walk through the
thorny desolate NOW.

She also says that faith is . . .

. . . Speaking the truth in love
even at the cost of
position
or relationship.[3]

If you need the Lord to give you faith to speak the truth in love to your family, ask Him now. And remember, though storms may follow, they are never out of His loving and caring control.

3. Pamela Reeve, *Faith Is . . .* (Sisters, Oreg.: Multnomah Books, 1994), n.p.

Chapter 7

FREEDOM FROM BONDAGE

Luke 8:26–39

Hollywood has tried to fashion our imaginations into a mausoleum of occultic images. Demonic monsters rise from the nether-world to drag human victims into their nightmarish realm. Seances summon unearthly winds that snuff out candles, leaving characters and audiences in oppressive and frightening darkness. Clerics fran-tically attempt to exorcise unruly spirits from ashen-faced victims.

These dramatizations exploit for profit our darker curiosities and fears. But they're just one slice of the deathly pie. Psychics and mediums claim to possess a sort of press pass into the spirit world, and for a fee, they'll provide you any "inside information" you need. *Power* can be yours, slick promoters say, if you can only tap into what lies beyond.

Both these approaches have led many people toward two ex-tremes concerning demons:

> One is to disbelieve in their existence. The other is
> to believe, and to feel an excessive and unhealthy
> interest in them. [The demons] themselves are
> equally pleased by both errors, and hail a materialist
> or a magician with the same delight.[1]

We can avoid these extremes by bypassing the media's celluloid portrayal of demons and looking to the pages of Scripture, where we'll find a solid description of our spiritual foes. The truth may send chills down our spines, but it may also give us the backbone to stand up to Satan's forces and their diabolical schemes.

Some Clarifying Remarks regarding Demons

Demons are not imaginary ghosts, fabricated in the minds of creative writers. Neither are they pointy-tailed characters perched

---

Sections of this chapter have been adapted from the chapter "What Is Your Name?" in the study guide, *Issues and Answers in Jesus' Day*, coauthored by Ken Gire, from the Bible-teaching ministry of Charles R. Swindoll (Fullerton, Calif.: Insight for Living, 1990), pp. 51–61.

1. C. S. Lewis, *The Screwtape Letters* with *Screwtape Proposes a Toast* (New York, N. Y.: Macmillan Publishing Co., 1959), p. 3.

on someone's shoulder in a comic strip. They are real but invisible creatures, powerful but not all-powerful.

Demons are the devious, insidious servants of Satan, the ruler of this world. And just like him, they are limited in their authority. In contrast, Christians are the servants of the unlimited, omnipotent God of the universe. We have no reason to feel afraid, victimized, or intimidated by demons (see 1 John 4:4).

But we do need to exercise caution. Paul told the stubborn believers in Corinth to forgive a repentant brother so that

> no advantage be taken of us by Satan; for we are
> not ignorant of his schemes. (2 Cor. 2:11)

A sustained, unforgiving, judgmental spirit invites Satan's influence because it's like leaving the door to our minds open; a demon can easily invade with thoughts of bitterness or pride. The Greek word for *schemes*, in fact, is related to the word for *mind*. Paul says, "We are not ignorant of Satan's mind games. We know his style." His emissaries will take every opportunity to influence our thinking.

Do you see how different this image of demons is from Hollywood's? Demons aren't hobgoblins, jumping at us from behind the bushes or setting up squatter's rights in our basements. They're much more subtle than that. Their purpose isn't to frighten us; their purpose is to destroy us from the inside out.

Jesus and the Demonized Victim

Turning to Luke 8, we encounter one of the most vivid and gripping portraits of evil in the entire Bible. The first person we meet in this account is more than influenced by the Devil; he's the Devil's prisoner.

The Setting

> And they sailed to the country of the Gerasenes,
> which is opposite Galilee. And when He had come
> out onto the land, He was met by a certain man from
> the city who was possessed with demons; and who
> had not put on any clothing for a long time, and was
> not living in a house, but in the tombs. (vv. 26–27)

In verse 29, Luke also tells us that Jesus

> had been commanding the unclean spirit to come

out of the man. For it had seized him many times; and he was bound with chains and shackles and kept under guard; and yet he would burst his fetters and be driven by the demon into the desert.

This graphic picture is hard to look at. Barely a vestige of humanity remains as the man roams about the tombs like an animal, naked and wild.

The man was *demonized,* hopelessly and helplessly under the domination of demonic powers.[2] His body was so controlled by satanic influences that it was merely a base of operation for the demons. Even his vocal chords were under their control.

The Dialogue

And seeing Jesus, he cried out and fell before Him, and said in a loud voice, "What do I have to do with You, Jesus, Son of the Most High God? I beg You, do not torment me." . . . And Jesus asked him, "What is your name?" And he said, "Legion";[3] for many demons had entered him. And they were entreating Him not to command them to depart into the abyss. (vv. 28, 30–31)

In an ongoing exchange, the demons keep "entreating" while Jesus keeps "commanding" (v. 29). The entrenchment of evil was so tenacious that uprooting it took more than one command, even from Jesus.

It's also interesting to note how much theology these demons knew. They knew that Jesus was the Son of the Most High God and that His power was greater than theirs. The apostle James reiterates these facts: "The demons also believe, and shudder" (James 2:19). Terrified of Jesus, they beg Him not to *torment* them. The Greek

2. *Demonized* is a term preferable to *demon-possessed.* "Confusion has been introduced by translating this participle as 'demon possessed.' The word *possession* implies ownership. Actually, demons own nothing. The New Testament regards them as squatters or invaders of territory that does not belong to them. In reality God owns *them,* for He is their Creator and their Judge. Such a faulty translation, then, misleads people regarding the state of the demonized person and causes undue consternation and terror in the hearts of the afflicted and those concerned for him." C. Fred Dickason, *Demon Possession and the Christian* (Chicago, Ill.: Moody Press, 1987), p. 38.

3. The number of soldiers in a Roman legion was around six thousand. According to Mark 5:13, there were about two thousand pigs in the herd; therefore, there could have been between two thousand and six thousand or more demons within this man.

word means "to examine by torture."[4] To them, Christ's presence on earth could mean that judgment was near. For they knew one more piece of theology: their final destiny, "the abyss."

The "abyss" they feared was the hellish bottomless pit reserved for Satan and his hordes during the Millennium (see Rev. 20:1–3 and the "Panoramic Survey of Satan" at the end of this chapter). Anything was better than that awful fate. So, trembling, the demons pleaded with Jesus not to judge them before the appointed time (see Matt. 8:29), and seeing a large herd of pigs feeding nearby, they "entreated Him to permit them to enter the swine" (Luke 8:32).

The Deliverance

Always subject to Jesus, the demons could not proceed until He allowed them to. At His nod, they

> came out from the man and entered the swine; and
> the herd rushed down the steep bank into the lake,
> and were drowned. (v. 33)

Mark's gospel tells us that "about two thousand" animals were hurled violently to their death after the demons entered them (5:13). Demons, remember, are not content merely to indwell and control; wherever they go, their purpose is to wreak havoc and destruction. So be wary. Don't let them put their foot in the door of your mind through occult books, movies, games, or trinkets. If you own some of these things, get rid of them—if you can, burn them, as the believers in Ephesus did (see Acts 19:19).

At the same time, we shouldn't become spiritually paranoid. Gremlins aren't hiding inside every CD case or lurking around every movie theater. Not all evil thoughts are demon-inspired. Nor are demons responsible for every emotional crisis or physical illness. It takes keen spiritual discernment to know whether an evil spirit is on the loose in our lives or if we are simply suffering the fallout of living in a sinful world. Jesus' example, though, reminds us that we must always be ready for spiritual battle—fully equipped to engage the enemy in Jesus' name.

The Results

The healing of the demoniac caused quite a stir. The entire

4. G. Abbott-Smith, *A Manual Greek Lexicon of the New Testament*, 3d ed. (Edinburgh, Scotland: T. and T. Clark, 1937), p. 76.

herd of pigs was lost, the herdsmen telegraphed the story to everyone they could find (Luke 8:34), and soon people came running to see what had happened (v. 35a). What they found amazed and frightened them.

> And they came to Jesus, and found the man from whom the demons had gone out, sitting down at the feet of Jesus, clothed and in his right mind; and they became frightened. And those who had seen it reported to them how the man who was demon-possessed had been made well. And all the people of the country of the Gerasenes and the surrounding district asked Him to depart from them; for they were gripped with great fear; and He got into a boat, and returned. (vv. 35b–37)

Where was gratitude for this desperate man's miraculous deliverance? Perhaps a lunatic restored to life and two thousand dead pigs were too much evidence of a power the people didn't care to reckon with. Sadly, they would rather push Jesus away than risk Him changing their lives too.

They couldn't deny that the man's life was changed. He was no longer out of control, but sitting calmly; he was no longer naked, but clothed; he was no longer crazy, but in his right mind. As Jesus and the disciples climbed back into the boat to leave, he started pleading with Jesus again—but this time it wasn't the demons imploring Jesus to let them be. This time the man was talking.

> But the man from whom the demons had gone out was begging Him that he might accompany Him; but He sent him away, saying, "Return to your house and describe what great things God has done for you." And he went away, proclaiming throughout the whole city what great things Jesus had done for him. (vv. 38–39)

What a transformation Jesus brought this man—from being a prisoner of darkness to becoming an ambassador of the Light!

Some Closing Observations and Suggestions

We've learned in this study that demons are neither funny nor phony. Since we all must deal with them at one time or another, we would be wise to keep in mind the following four words of counsel.

First, *expect struggles with the enemy.* Don't be "ignorant of his schemes" (2 Cor. 2:11; see also Eph. 6:12). Second, *stand firm in the full armor of God* (see Eph. 6:11, 13–18). Third, as James advises, *resist the enemy by the power of the Spirit* (James 4:7). And fourth, *never forget that only believers are on the winning side.* Martin Luther assures us with his victorious hymn, *A Mighty Fortress Is Our God,*

> And though this world with devils filled,
> Should threaten to undo us,
> We will not fear, for God hath willed
> His truth to triumph through us.
> The prince of darkness grim,
> We tremble not for him—
> His rage we can endure,
> For lo, his doom is sure:
> One little word shall fell him.[5]

And that Word is Jesus.

 Living Insights

Is it easier for you to trust Christ in the natural or the supernatural realm? To put it another way: Which worries you more, the visible things that go awry during the day? Or the invisible things that go bump in the night?

According to author Ken Gire, it's not by accident that Jesus' encounter with the Gerasene demoniac comes on the heels of His encounter with the stormy sea.

> His fledgling students have just learned that Jesus is Lord over the natural realm. In this sequel to that lesson, they will learn that he is also Lord over the supernatural realm. And they will observe firsthand that he can calm a tormented soul as easily as he calmed a tempestuous sea.[6]

5. Martin Luther, "A Mighty Fortress Is Our God," in *Hymns for the Family of God* (Nashville, Tenn.: Paragon Associates, 1976), no. 118.

6. Ken Gire, *Intimate Moments with the Savior: Learning to Love* (Grand Rapids, Mich.: Zondervan Publishing House, 1989), p. 39.

Physical or metaphysical, normal or paranormal—Christ is Lord over it all. Because of this fact, Neil Anderson, in *The Bondage Breaker*, writes that we can remain calm when we feel targeted by demons.

> John promised, "Greater is He who is in you than he who is in the world" (1 John 4:4). You have authority over Satan's activity and you have the armor of God to protect you. Whenever Satan attacks, you must "be strong in the Lord, and in the strength of His might" (Ephesians 6:10). Consciously place yourself in the Lord's hands, resist Satan with the spoken Word. . . . You are only vulnerable when you are walking by sight instead of by faith or walking in the flesh instead of in the Spirit.[7]

In light of our study, how will you handle those spine-tingling brushes with the forces of darkness that we all sense from time to time?

_____

_____

_____

_____

 Living Insights STUDY TWO

Concerning Satan's more subtle attacks, Neil Anderson gives us a sobering warning:

> Even though our eternal destiny is secure and the armor of God is readily available, we are still vulnerable to Satan's accusations, temptations, and deceptions. If we give in to these, we can be influenced by Satan's wishes (Galatians 5:1). And if we remain under his influence long enough, we can lose control. Yes, believers can be controlled by Satan if they fail to stand against him. *Ownership* is never at stake, however. We belong to God, and Satan can't

---

7. Neil T. Anderson, *The Bondage Breaker* (Eugene, Oreg.: Harvest House Publishers, 1990), p. 102.

touch our basic identity in Him. But as long as we are living in this body, we can allow ourselves to be vulnerable targets to all his fiery darts.[8]

What are some fiery darts Satan has been flinging at you in the three areas that Anderson mentions?

Accusations _____

_____

Temptations _____

_____

Deceptions _____

_____

To defend against these attacks, we own several pieces of spiritual armor (see Eph. 6:10–18). How can each piece help you fend off Satan's darts in the specific areas mentioned above?

The Belt of Truth _____

_____

The Breastplate of Righteousness _____

_____

The Boots of the Gospel _____

_____

The Shield of Faith _____

_____

The Helmet of Salvation _____

_____

The Sword of the Spirit _____

8. Anderson, *The Bondage Breaker*, p. 99.

Prayer _____

 Digging Deeper _____

Step-by-Step Instructions for Gaining Deliverance

On certain occasions the Christian may find it necessary to take direct action against Satan and his evil spirits. The technique involved to carry out such action is not complicated. James 4:7 says:

> Submit therefore to God. Resist the devil and he will flee from you.

This "resistance" action may be done as follows:

1. Openly and orally declare your faith in the Lord Jesus Christ. This announcement should be uttered aloud and with deep conviction.

2. Destroy every trinket, reminder, and attachment you may have in your possession that is associated with the occult or satanic system. Burning is the biblical method of destruction (Acts 19:19).

3. Confess your sins of involvement and/or association with the powers of darkness—naming them one by one. Claim your deliverance through the power of:
   a. The Word of God (Eph. 6:17; Heb. 4:12)
   b. The Name of the *Lord* Jesus Christ (Phil. 2:9–10; Col. 3:17)
   c. The Blood of the Lord (Rev. 12:11)
   d. The Cross of Calvary (Col. 2:13–15; Heb. 2:14–15)

4. Reclaim the ground in your life that the enemy has been allowed to control. Do this by going back over your life, mentally, asking the Holy Spirit to bring to your remembrance any and all ground (areas) through which the enemy might yet hold some advantage over you. As each individual area is brought to light, *declare aloud* that you reclaim it in the name of the Lord Jesus Christ, through the power of His blood. By doing so you cancel and annul your having given ground to the Devil.

5. Close the session with a prayer that goes something like this: "*I do here and now renounce and refuse any and all allegiance I have ever given to Satan and his hosts of wicked spirits. I refuse to be influenced by them, and I refuse to be used by them in any way whatsoever. I reject all their attacks upon my mind, my spirit, my soul, and my body. I claim the shed blood of the Lord Jesus Christ upon every circumference of my being, and I revoke all their power and influence with me or around about me. I resist them in the name of my Lord and Savior Jesus Christ. I plead the merits of that transaction upon the Cross of Calvary whereby Satan and all his powers became defeated foes through the blood of the Lord Jesus Christ. I stand upon the promises in the Word of God. In humble faith I do here and now put on the whole armor of God, and in doing so I am able to stand against all the schemes of the Devil.*"

This chart is limited to actual accounts of demonic contact

Scripture	Victim	Tormentor	Victim's Experience
Matthew 4:24	Unnamed sick people.	Demon.	Demonized.
Matthew 8:16 Mark 1:32–34 Luke 4:40–41	Many who were demonized and sick.	Demon, spirit.	Demonized.
Matthew 8:28–34 Mark 5:1–20 Luke 8:26–39	A certain man.	Demons— unclean spirits named Legion.	Demonized. Lived near tombs. Naked. Super-human strength. No rest. Seizures. Suicidal attacks. No restraint.
Matthew 9:32–33	"A dumb man."	Demon.	Demonized. Unable to speak.
Matthew 12:22	A man.	Demon.	Demonized. Blind and dumb.
Matthew 15:22–28 Mark 7:24–30	A Gentile woman's daughter.	Demon, unclean spirit.	Cruelly demonized.
Matthew 17:14–20 Mark 9:14–29 Luke 9:37–43	A man's only son.	Spirit, demon, unclean spirit.	Mute. Very ill. Suicidal. Seizures. Convulsions. Screaming. Had this "from childhood."
Mark 1:23–27 Luke 4:31–35	"A man."	Unclean spirit, unclean demon.	Cried out. Demon knew Jesus as "Jesus of Nazareth . . . the Holy One of God."
Mark 3:10–11	Many who had afflictions.	Unclean spirits.	Unclean spirits beheld Jesus and cried out: "You are the Son of God!"
Mark 16:9 Luke 8:2	"Some women," Mary Magdalene.	Demons, evil spirits.	Mary had seven demons.

NOTE: There are two descriptive titles used to denote the presence of Satan's workers. One is *demon*, which is from a Greek word meaning "knowing" or "intelligence." A demon is a "knowing one." Intelligence is the most prominent characteristic among demons. Their superior knowledge is used to frustrate God's work and also serves to attract the interest of humans. The other title is *spirit*, which tells us that demons do not possess a material body of flesh and bones (see Luke 24:39). They are, however, able to enter in and assume control

THE NEW TESTAMENT

with humans for the purpose of affliction and torment.

Method Used to Expel Demons	Demons' Response	Final Result
Jesus "healed them."		Healing.
Laid hands on victims. Cast out with a word. Rebuked the demons.	Cried out, "You are the Son of God!"	Healing.
Talked with demons. Asked for name—"Legion." "Come out . . . , you unclean spirit!" "Begone!" Granted demons' request.	Knew Jesus was the Son of God. Requested to enter swine. Came out and entered swine.	Complete relief. Clothed, resting. In right mind. (Swine drowned.)
Demon was "cast out."		Man was able to speak.
"He healed him."		Man was able to speak and see.
"Healed at once." (Daughter was not present.)	Departed.	Child was lying on her bed. The demon was gone.
Rebuked unclean spirit. Healed the boy. "I command you, come out . . . do not enter him again!"	Cried out. Threw victim into terrible convulsions, departed.	The boy was cured at once. Became quiet "like a corpse."
Jesus rebuked him: "Be quiet and come out of him!"	Threw victim down, caused him convulsions, but did no harm to victim. Came out.	Complete relief.
He healed many.	Fell down before Him.	Healing.
Cast out; healed of evil spirits.		Healing.

Chart continued on next page

of a human body, speaking and acting through it from time to time. This title also tells us that demons are not normally subject to human visibility or other sensory perceptions. Their invisibility makes their presence insidious and hard to detect. The word *evil* denotes labor, pain, and sorrow—that which is destructive and injurious. The term *unclean* denotes impurity, filthiness, and defilement.

Demon Contact in the New Testament—*Continued*

Scripture	Victim	Tormentor	Victim's Experience
Luke 6:17–18	Great throng of people.	Unclean spirits.	Troubled.
Luke 7:21	Many people.	Evil spirits.	
Luke 11:14–26	A man.	Demon, unclean spirit.	Mute—unable to speak.
Luke 13:10–17	A woman— "a daughter of Abraham."	Spirit.	"A sickness caused by a spirit . . . bent double, and could not straighten up at all." Lasted eighteen years.
Acts 5:16	People who were afflicted.	Unclean spirits.	Affliction.
Acts 8:7	Many people.	Unclean spirits.	
Acts 13:6–11*	A certain magician, Bar-Jesus.		Sought to turn another away from the faith.
Acts 16:16–18	"A certain slave-girl."	"A spirit of divination."	Persistent crying out, hindering the gospel.
Acts 19:11–16	Unnamed individuals, a man.	Evil spirit.	Violent, superhuman strength.

*This person is not specifically described as having a demon, but the pattern seems very similar to that of demonic contact.

Method Used to Expel Demons	Demons' Response	Final Result
"Being cured."		Cured.
"Cured."		Cured.
"Casting out."		"The dumb man spoke."
Laid hands on her. "Woman, you are freed from your sickness."		Immediately she was made erect, glorified God, and was healed.
		Healing.
	"They were coming out of them shouting with a loud voice."	Healing.
Severe, sudden rebuke by Paul. Blindness pronounced.		The other person believed in Christ.
Paul rebuked it: "I command you in the name of Jesus Christ to come out of her!"	Instantly came out.	Girl was released and was no longer able to tell fortunes.
Unqualified men, the "seven sons of one Sceva, a Jewish high priest," tried to cast out the evil spirit.	Evil spirit recognized Jesus and Paul, but not these men. The demonized man leaped on and overpowered all seven men.	The "deliverers" fled, naked and wounded.

Panoramic Survey of Satan

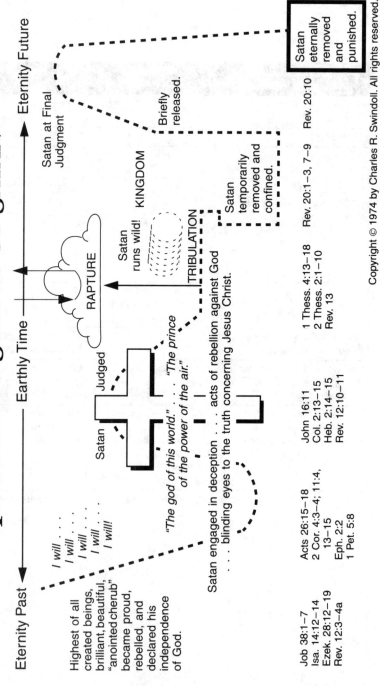

Eternity Past — Earthly Time — Eternity Future

I will . . . .
I will . . . .
I will . . . .
I will . . . .
I will!

Highest of all created beings, brilliant, beautiful, "anointed cherub" became proud, rebelled, and declared his independence of God.

"The god of this world" . . . "The prince of the power of the air."

Satan — Judged

RAPTURE

Satan runs wild!

TRIBULATION

KINGDOM

Satan at Final Judgment

Briefly released.

Satan temporarily removed and confined.

Satan eternally removed and punished.

Satan engaged in deception . . . acts of rebellion against God . . . blinding eyes to the truth concerning Jesus Christ.

Job 38:1–7
Isa. 14:12–14
Ezek. 28:12–19
Rev. 12:3–4a

Acts 26:15–18
2 Cor. 4:3–4; 11:4, 13–15
Eph. 2:2
1 Pet. 5:8

John 16:11
Col. 2:13–15
Heb. 2:14–15
Rev. 12:10–11

1 Thess. 4:13–18
2 Thess. 2:1–10
Rev. 13

Rev. 20:1–3, 7–9

Rev. 20:10

Chapter 8

NEVER TOO LITTLE . . .
NEVER TOO LOST

Luke 8:40–56

What is it about Jesus that people would leave family and friends to follow Him? That martyrs would die rather than deny Him? That the Mother Teresas of the world would give their lives loving the unlovely in His name? What is it about Him that stirs such passionate devotion?

In his book *Jesus, Man of Joy*, Sherwood Wirt admits that, according to the world's standard of greatness, Jesus' life wasn't that extraordinary.

> From a strictly materialistic viewpoint, this Person's active life did not accomplish all that much. Remarkable actions were attributed to Him, but He wrote no epics and raised no monuments. In early youth He seems to have worked with His hands. Later He taught, prayed, and healed, as many prophets had done before Him and have done since. That He had noble character and personal charm, and uttered many wise things that people have been quoting ever since, could be said also of others.
>
> Yet for this Person to be endowed with such universal appeal, there must have been something very special about Him. The world has never forgotten Him. His name is on someone's lips every second of time; in fact, time is dated from His birth. A billion human beings today claim to be His followers, and most of them are convinced that He is the Author of their personal salvation.
>
> But if there was "something special" about Him, what was it?[1]

What was it, indeed?

---

1. Sherwood Eliot Wirt, *Jesus, Man of Joy* (San Bernardino, Calif.: Here's Life Publishers, 1991), pp. 15–16.

Some of the Things We Admire Most about Christ

Here are just a few of the many reasons we are attracted to Jesus. First, He accomplished what He came to do. He was a finisher. We respect people who live what they say.

Second, we admire Him because He saw beyond what people were and affirmed what they could become. Take rough-edged Peter, for example. Jesus saw him not as a crumbling failure who denied Him three times but as the "rock" who would one day form the foundation of His church (see Matt. 16:18).

Third, He remained joyful and positive in spite of the obstacles. Although squeezed in the vise of intense suffering, He never expressed bitterness or rancor. He epitomized the art of living above one's circumstances.

Finally, we admire Jesus' heart of compassion—perhaps His most appealing quality of all. People mattered to Him. When He was on earth, He took time to listen. To welcome a child. To touch a leper. To mingle His tears with the tears of the grieving. To Him, no one was too little or too lost—not even a dying young girl or a frail, despairing woman.

Two Examples of His Heart of Compassion

Where the people of the Gerasenes couldn't wait for Jesus to leave, the Galileans could hardly wait for Him to step ashore. One distraught father in particular was especially anxious for Jesus' arrival.

A Little Girl Who Needed Life

> And as Jesus returned, the multitude welcomed Him, for they had all been waiting for Him. And behold, there came a man named Jairus, and he was an official of the synagogue; and he fell at Jesus' feet, and began to entreat Him to come to his house; for he had an only daughter, about twelve years old, and she was dying. But as He went, the multitudes were pressing against Him. (Luke 8:40–42)

As a synagogue official, according to William Barclay, Jairus was

> responsible for the administration of the synagogue and the ordering of public worship. He had reached the highest post that life could give him in the respect of his fellow-men. No doubt he was well to

do; no doubt he had climbed the ladder of earthly ambition and prestige. It seemed as if life—as it sometimes does—had given lavishly of many things but was about to take the most precious thing away.[2]

Death is no respecter of persons or position. Jairus' good standing in the community, his success, and his money were all powerless to stem the tide of darkness that was slowly ebbing over his only daughter. Casting aside all pride, he fell on his face at Jesus' feet, desperately grasping for one last lifeline for his little girl.

Without a word, Jesus sets out for the man's house. For our Savior is not One to announce His compassion: "Miracle today! Follow Me!" Nor does He tell Jairus to bring his daughter back at two o'clock for an appointment. He simply goes.

Along the way, more people join the crowd, and the mob becomes a swirling current that pushes and jostles Jesus down the road. Everyone's attention is on Jesus and Jairus and the approaching miracle, when, unnoticed, another hand of faith quietly reaches out of the sea of humanity to Jesus.

A Lost Woman Who Needed Hope

And a woman who had a hemorrhage for twelve years, and could not be healed by anyone, came up behind Him, and touched the fringe of His cloak;[3] and immediately her hemorrhage stopped. (vv. 43–44)

For as many years as the little girl has brought light into Jairus' family, this woman has suffered alone in darkness. For twelve humiliating years, she has tried cure after cure—most of them painful and degrading. Mark says that she

had endured much at the hands of many physicians, and had spent all that she had and was not helped at all, but rather had grown worse. (Mark 5:26)

2. William Barclay, *The Gospel of Luke*, rev. ed., The Daily Study Bible Series (Philadelphia, Pa.: Westminster Press, 1975), p. 110.

3. According to G. Campbell Morgan, "We get nearer to the meaning of the verb if we use the word, clutched. She did not merely put her hand out, and touch. She grasped . . . the tassel" which Moses had commanded be sewn on the corners of the Jews' garments (see Num. 15:37–41). *The Gospel according to Luke* (Westwood, N.J.: Fleming H. Revell Co., 1931), p. 116.

At the hands of society she has endured even more. Classified as "unclean," she is not allowed to touch or be touched by anyone. Ken Gire, in *Intimate Moments with the Savior*, describes the woman as you would have seen her on the street.

> Her eyes are downcast as you pass by. She is self-conscious . . . ashamed . . . and afraid. She fears the condescension in your eyes. She fears the indifference of your shoulder turned coldly against her. But most of all, she fears the gavel you bring down on her life. She fears the rapped judgment that her illness is the direct result of some personal sin. And with a bleeding uterus, anyone could guess what kind of sin she has committed. "Sexual, no doubt," are the whispered innuendos. "Some perversion, most likely," are the gossiped indictments.[4]

Her resources spent, her dreams in ashes, she hears about the one Person who could help her. The Great Physician. He's kind. He's gentle. He's compassionate. If she could just touch Him, maybe . . .

At once, an overwhelming power rushes through her body, and she lets go, falling back into the stream of rushing people. So eager to see a miracle, the crowd overlooks one performed right in their midst. Jesus, however, doesn't miss a thing.

> And Jesus said, "Who is the one who touched Me?" And while they were all denying it, Peter said, "Master, the multitudes are crowding and pressing upon You." But Jesus said, "Someone did touch Me, for I was aware that power had gone out of Me." (Luke 8:45–46)

Wait a minute. Jesus doesn't have time to stop. He's on an emergency call. Jairus has dialed 911; the ambulance is racing; the sirens are screaming. But Jesus suddenly slams on the brakes: "Who touched Me?"

Peter is incredulous. "Who *didn't* touch you?" he replies. But hiding somewhere in the crowd, a certain woman knows exactly what Jesus means.

---

4. Ken Gire, *Intimate Moments with the Savior* (Grand Rapids, Mich.: Zondervan Publishing House, 1989), p. 47.

> And when the woman saw that she had not escaped
> notice, she came trembling and fell down before
> Him, and declared in the presence of all the people
> the reason why she had touched Him, and how she
> had been immediately healed. And He said to her,
> "Daughter, your faith has made you well; go in
> peace." (vv. 47–48)

The outcast woman fears further embarrassment, but what she
hears from Jesus are the kindest words she's heard in twelve years:
"Daughter . . . well . . . peace."

While a fire of hope warms this woman's soul, though, the light
of life has flickered and died in the soul of another daughter.

> While He was still speaking, someone came from
> the house of the synagogue official, saying, "Your
> daughter has died; do not trouble the Teacher any-
> more." (v. 49)

The message hits Jairus with a crushing blow. They were so
close! How could this happen? The woman's faith made her well,
but what about *his* faith? What about *his* daughter? Unlike the
woman, her whole life was ahead of her. If Jesus hadn't stopped,
she would have had a chance at living that life. But now she is gone.

Jesus reads the confusion and pain in Jairus' eyes and says,

> "Do not be afraid any longer; only believe, and she
> shall be made well." (v. 50b)

Not wanting God's mercy to become a sideshow, Jesus takes
only Jairus and his wife, and Peter, James, and John with Him as
He goes to the girl. Then He gets things quiet and under control.

> Now they were all weeping and lamenting for her;
> but He said, "Stop weeping, for she has not died,
> but is asleep." And they began laughing at Him,
> knowing that she had died. He, however, took her
> by the hand and called, saying, "Child, arise!" And
> her spirit returned, and she rose immediately; and
> He gave orders for something to be given her to eat.
> And her parents were amazed; but He instructed
> them to tell no one what had happened. (vv. 52–56)

Here's another reason we love Jesus: for His humility. "This

69

miracle is just for you. Don't tell anyone." Mostly, though, we love Him for His compassionate touch—the touch of life He offers to all who follow Him.

The Next Time You Feel "Too Busy"

Can you imagine the mourners' surprise when the girl emerged from the room, alive and hungry for lunch? They had already signed the death certificate. Plans for the burial were being made. But Jesus said, "Not so fast. I still have work to do here."

When we get ahead of the Lord, there are three things we need to *realize, refuse,* and *remember.*

Realize that all of life is directed by the Lord, not just the part we have planned. Even the things we're sure about aren't set in stone. *Refuse* to discount the unexpected interruptions. God's timing is in no way linked to the human clock. And some things we view as annoying interruptions may actually be divine interventions. And *remember* that being too busy tends to make us talk too much. Jesus told the girl's parents, Peter, James, and John not to tell anyone what happened in the room. Scoffing mourners don't need to know everything. Sometimes the richest treasures God gives a family should be reserved in a vault of cherished memories.

 Living Insights

How great a debt we owe the gospel writers, who not only tell us what Jesus did, but what He felt. From the following verses, what are some of the circumstances that moved Jesus to compassion?

Matthew 9:36 _____

14:14 _____

15:32 _____

Mark 1:40–42 _____

10:17–23 _____

Luke 7:12–13 _____

John 11:30–38 _____

Are you wounded? Are you grieving? Are you struggling with

your faith? One of the reasons God sent His Son was so we could see His tears. Our sorrow breaks the heart of God. And, although He may not bring back our loved ones from behind the veil of death or heal us in an instant, He has a special touch waiting for us. A touch of assurance. Of hope. Of peace.

Won't you receive His touch today?

> Let us therefore draw near with confidence to the throne of grace, that we may receive mercy and may find grace to help in time of need. (Heb. 4:16)

 Living Insights

Sometimes in our heartache, we withdraw into ourselves. We go through the motions of prayer, of service, of worship, but we never fall at His feet, never cling to His robe. We brush by the Lord like we brush by the minister on the way to the parking lot.

If you've felt yourself drawing back from the Lord, read Ken Gire's prayer from *Intimate Moments with the Savior*. Make it your own, as you pause right now to reach out to our compassionate Lord.

Dear Most Merciful of Physicians,

> Help me to realize that it was not the healthy who reached out to you. They bunched up in crowds, but it was those who suffered greatly who reached out to grasp you.
>
> It was the people in the streets, not in the sitting rooms of society, that groped for your garment. It was needy people. People with outstretched arms. People with empty hands. People who had nothing to offer but the faith that you could make them whole.
>
> I confess, O Lord, how often I have followed in the crowd pressed around you. Yet how few times have those brushes with you changed my life. I have touched you, but only in the rush hour of religious activity.
>
> Sunday after Sunday I take my part in the crowd as I sit through the service. I repeat the liturgy, sing

the hymns, hear the sermon. I read my Bible, say my prayers, give my money. I attend the right seminars, tune in the right programs, read the right books.

How could I be so close to your presence yet so far from your power?

Could it be that my arms are folded? Could it be that my hands are full?

I pray that if my arms are complacent, you would unfold them in outstretched longing for you. And if my hands are full, I pray that you would empty them so that I might cling only to you.[5]

5. Gire, *Intimate Moments with the Savior*, p. 51.

Chapter 9

SECRETS OF A LASTING MINISTRY

Luke 9:1–11

Exhilarating . . . fulfilling . . . agonizing. That's the way most pastors would describe full-time ministry. They love serving the Lord and helping others. They treasure the challenge of handling a variety of responsibilities and the satisfaction that their work counts for more than just a paycheck.

But with the occupational joys come the hazards. The pay is low. The hours are long. The frustrations are many. According to a recent survey, one out of every two pastors feels unable to meet the needs of the job. Ninety percent of them lament that their training was insufficient for their position. And most battle feelings of loneliness, isolation, and inadequacy.[1] One other study revealed a further telling statistic: the average tenure of a senior pastor in a church is about four years.[2]

The early church leaders certainly had their ups and downs too. Even Peter tasted failure's bitter cup the day he denied the Lord. However, except for Judas, the disciples seemed to possess a staying power that carried them through the tough times. What helped them stick with it to the end, even to martyrdom?

To find the answer to this question, we must begin not with them but with their Mentor.

Remembering Jesus' Unique Mission

Undergirding each of the early church leaders was a life-changing encounter with Jesus Christ. Paul recorded a first-century Christian hymn that explains the nature of our amazing Lord.

> He who was revealed in the flesh,
> Was vindicated in the Spirit,
> Beheld by angels,

---

1. Based on an article by Rolf Zettersten, "Ministering to Your Pastor," *Focus on the Family* magazine, January 1993, p. 14.

2. George Barna, *Today's Pastors* (Ventura, Calif.: Gospel Light, Regal Books, 1993), p. 36.

Proclaimed among the nations,
Believed on in the world,
Taken up in glory. (1 Tim. 3:16b)

Into the vellum of this ancient theological statement we can stamp four words that sum up Jesus' life: He *came*, He *chose*, He *died*, He *departed*. Revealing Himself in human flesh through the virgin birth, He *came* as the incarnate Son of God. After His vindication by the Spirit at His baptism, He *chose* the twelve disciples. During His three years of ministry, He was beheld, proclaimed, and believed in, then He *died* as an atonement for sin—the goal of His mission on earth. Finally, "taken up in glory," He *departed* this world, saying that one day He would return to collect His own.

Knowing that He would eventually leave the earth, Jesus needed to prepare a group of leaders who would carry on His mission after He was gone. And, thanks to Luke, we can see Him in action, training His men for lasting ministry.

Getting the Twelve Launched into Ministry

In Luke's first-century "training video," he shows us four scenes illustrating guidelines for leaders.

Essential Equipment

First, we see Jesus giving the disciples the equipment for serving Him.

> And He called the twelve together, and gave them power and authority over all the demons, and to heal diseases. And He sent them out to proclaim the kingdom of God, and to perform healing. (Luke 9:1–2)

According to these verses, the first two tools in any minister's work belt are Christ's *power* and *authority*. Scripture tells us that at the moment of salvation, we receive the power of God—the Holy Spirit (see Eph. 1:13–14). Pulsating within us is the irresistible, irreplaceable, supernatural power of God's very Spirit. This power is not seen—unlike authority, which is visible and tangible.

A minister with Christ's power and authority is like a traffic cop who, by simply raising a hand, can bring two tons of speeding automobile to a complete halt. Does the officer have the power to stop the car? No, but the authority of the uniform does; it is respected because it's backed by the law. In a similar way, a minister's authority is backed by the power of the Holy Spirit. There's a balance between what we do and what God does through us. We use our insights and gifts, but His power gets the work done.

The second set of tools are also ones that ministers must use together and in balance: *proclaiming* and *performing*. The Greek word for *proclaim* is *kērussō*, which means "to be a herald." As King of creation, Jesus pronounced the message; the disciples merely heralded His royal decree. The influence rested not in their polished oratory or their impressive exposition but in the message they delivered and the Person it was from.

A ministry will not last when there is no clear, consistent, faithful message based on the Word of God. A pastor must be a herald of the truth if the work is to endure.

To validate the disciples' message, Jesus gave them the ability "to perform healing." Wherever they went, they were heralding and healing, teaching and caring, saying and doing. Their deeds of righteousness backed up their righteous teaching.

The Pharisees, in contrast, talked a good talk, but failed to support it with their lives. Jesus called them hypocrites. When kept in balance, the equipment of words and deeds will give a ministry direction and guard it against superficiality.

After equipping His disciples, Jesus gives them some realistic advice on ministry life, the place where the rubber meets the road.

Realistic Advice

> And He said to them, "Take nothing for your journey, neither a staff, nor a bag, nor bread, nor money; and do not even have two tunics apiece. And whatever house you enter, stay there, and take your leave from there. And as for those who do not receive you, as you go out from that city, shake off the dust from your feet as a testimony against them." (Luke 9:3–5)

In other words, *travel light*. We walk quicker and farther with our arms free and our hands empty. When God says go, we're ready. No lagging behind because we're dragging a trunk full of extras. No stumbling because our arms are so full that we can't see the road in front of us.

Essentially, Jesus' message is this: "Don't become attached to your things. Keep your list of needs brief and simple." Does He mean that we shouldn't own things? No. We just shouldn't let things own us.

His second word of wisdom can be summed up this way: *toughen up*. According to William Barclay, rabbis returning to Jewish soil after journeying through gentile land used to shake off "the last particle of heathen dust from their feet."[3] Think of that "heathen dust" as unfair criticism. In ministry, our journey will inevitably take us down a path of swirling condemnation. Like the rabbis, we need to be able to shake the dirt from our feet and move on, to not put too much emphasis on those who don't receive our ministry.

Of course, a friend's firm hand on our shoulder and word of constructive reproof is a welcome correction. But the dust we're talking about is derogatory sarcasm, unsigned letters, or backhanded comments. Attempting to rectify these criticisms and trying to please every church member will quickly demoralize and derail us from our most important tasks.

There's a saying: "When a mule kicks you . . . consider the source." No doubt about it, kicks of criticism hurt. Pastors who persevere, though, are prepared for them. They maintain their sensitive hearts, but they also develop thick skin. Most importantly, they refuse to condemn themselves, because when that happens, Satan has surely won the victory.

Public Opinions

The next three verses are a historical sidelight, inserted here by Luke to set up the scene in chapter 23 where Jesus meets Herod Antipas face-to-face during one of His trials (see 23:8–12). However, woven into these verses is a pertinent issue—how to handle public opinion.

> Now Herod the tetrarch heard of all that was happening; and he was greatly perplexed, because it was said by some that John had risen from the dead, and by some that Elijah had appeared, and by others, that one of the prophets of old had risen again. And Herod said, "I myself had John beheaded; but who is this man about whom I hear such things?" And he kept trying to see Him. (9:7–9)

What judgments was the public opinion machine cranking out

3. William Barclay, *The Gospel of Luke*, rev. ed., The Daily Study Bible Series (Philadelphia, Pa.: Westminster Press, 1975), p. 115.

about Christ? "He is John the Baptizer, risen from the dead." "He is Elijah." And, "He is one of the prophets of old." Herod wasn't sure which to choose. His perceptions were based only on hearsay, because he had never met Jesus in person.

To Jesus, though, people's opinions didn't matter much. He had a job to do. And we have a job to do too. Worrying about what is being said about us will get us off track. We start becoming people pleasers and poll watchers rather than faithful servants of Christ.

Instead of playing for the crowd, stay real. Follow God's leading. And don't put much stock in your press reports. Charles Spurgeon once said,

> The highest reputation in the world is to be faithful—faithful to your God and your own conscience. As to the approbation of the unconverted multitude, or of worldly professors, do not care the turn of a button for it; it may be a deadly heritage. Many a man is more a slave to his admirers than he dreams of: the love of approbation is more a bondage than an inner dungeon would be. If you have done the right thing before God, and are not afraid of His great Judgment Seat, fear nothing, but go forward.[4]

Personal Accountability

In verses 10 and 11, Luke describes what happened when the apostles returned.

> They gave an account to Him of all that they had done. And taking them with Him, He withdrew by Himself to a city called Bethsaida. (v. 10)

This was a time just for Jesus and the disciples—a private time for encouragement and empathy, for evaluation and instruction, for Jesus to say, "I've been there; I understand."

One of the secrets of a lasting ministry is having time for honest, open interaction and evaluation with those more experienced. It will help you battle loneliness. It will give you staying power.

Oh, and one more thing Jesus modeled—gracious patience:

4. Charles Haddon Spurgeon, "Runaway Jonah and the Covenant Ship"—Jonah 1:3, *Metropolitan Tabernacle Pulpit* (Pasadena, Tex.: Pilgrim Publications, 1974), vol. 36, p. 591.

But the multitudes were aware of this and followed Him; and welcoming them, He began speaking to them about the kingdom of God and curing those who had need of healing. (v. 11)

Applying These Same Guidelines Today

At least four challenges arise from Jesus' training of the Twelve.

- *Take a look at your equipment.* Are you genuinely saved so that His power is backing you up? Do your deeds support your words? Have His tools in your life gotten rusty for lack of use?

- *Lighten up and get tough.* Release some of your excess baggage, shake the dust of criticism off your feet, and quit running scared of what people are going to think and say.

- *Pay the most attention to God's opinion.* Like a house of mirrors, others' opinions distort our view of ourselves. Only God shows us who we really are.

- *Invite the evaluation of those you trust and respect.* Be transparent. Reveal your dreams and disappointments to people you can trust. Let others help you stay focused on the basics of ministry: adoring and serving Christ.

 Living Insights STUDY ONE

Whether a pastor, a Sunday school teacher, or a community volunteer, we all hope for a fulfilling, lasting ministry. Often, however, the opposite occurs—like what happened to Margie.

Enthusiastic and a bit nervous, Margie accepted the nomination to head up the women's ministry at her church. For a while, she reveled in the challenge and enjoyed putting her vision into action. However, like thorns hiding in a bouquet of roses, some things about the ministry started snagging her joy. She noticed other people were sitting back, watching her do all the work. She also saw the toll her involvement was taking on her family. But, determined, she kept going. Then, without warning, a criticism jabbed her between the shoulder blades. A sarcastic remark pricked her arm. A cutting joke stabbed her in the stomach.

"This is painful!" she cried. Emotionally bleeding, she dragged herself to the end of her term, vowing never to volunteer for anything again, and settled into the ranks of the "sitters."

If you identify with Margie's story, you're not alone. The church is strewn with wounded leaders just like you, trying to understand what went wrong. If you haven't already, take some time now to work through your feelings.

As a result of your experience, does self-condemnation plague you? If so, in what way?

_____

_____

_____

How has your attitude changed toward people in the church?

_____

_____

_____

Have you spoken to anyone about your hurt feelings? Do you know a trusted, more experienced leader you could talk to? Who is this person?

_____

Have you spoken to the Lord about your experience? If not, pour out your discouragements and hurts to Him. If anyone understands what a wounded leader feels like, He does.

_____

_____

_____

_____

 Living Insights STUDY TWO

If you're ready to step into ministry again—or if you're currently in ministry or just thinking about it—use this Living Insight to help prepare you to face the challenges ahead.

Based on the guidelines from the lesson, write out the ways you intend to put these principles into action.

- I plan to rely on God's power and authority by _____

  _____

  _____

- I plan to balance the message I proclaim and the works I perform by

  _____

  _____

- I plan to loosen my grip on things so I can more freely serve the Lord by _____

  _____

  _____

- I plan to keep my heart sensitive and, at the same time, my skin tough toward criticism by_____

  _____

  _____

- I plan to pay more attention to God's opinion of me by_____

  _____

  _____

- I plan to seek evaluation from wise, experienced friends by __

  _____

  _____

Chapter 10
THE MIRACLE MEAL
Luke 9:12–17

For a child, the most ordinary of experiences can open a door to learning. For example, a three-year-old spies a silver trail on the sidewalk and squats down to ponder a snail inching by. Nose-to-antennae with the little creature, the child's mind whirls: *Where is it going? How does it move? What happens when you touch these two wiggly things sticking out the front?*

A wise parent will pause while the door is open to marvel with the child at the wonders of God's world. The teachable moment is now, not later. Any minute, the curiosity will wane. The opportunity will be lost.

Like a parent, God looks for those golden moments in our lives when we're attentive and willing to learn. They come during good times, when we're lifted to praise. During hard times, when difficulties yank us down. And most of all, they occur during impossible times, when we face a problem that defies a solution . . . when the numbers won't add up . . . when the walls won't come down . . . when only a miracle will do.

A Few Thoughts on the Miracles God Performs

The term *miracle* means something different to different people, so let's take a moment to understand precisely what it is.

What, Then, Is a Miracle?

We tend to toss the word around a lot, letting it tumble into situations in which it doesn't really belong. For instance, we say that the new life forming in a mother's womb is a "miracle." But conception is natural, not supernatural. Amazing, remarkable, phenomenal—yes. But not miraculous. Now, a baby conceived in the womb of a virgin, like Mary—*that* would be a miracle.

Miracles, then, are *supernatural interventions of God in which He*

Portions of this chapter have been adapted from the chapter "The Problem of Facing Impossibilities," in the study guide *You and Your Problems*, coauthored by Lee Hough, from the Bible-teaching ministry of Charles R. Swindoll (Fullerton, Calif.: Insight for Living, 1989), pp. 86–90.

interrupts natural laws for His own sovereign purposes. You only find miracles in impossible situations, where the wonder of nature stops and the power of deity begins. For example, it was impossible for the fleeing Hebrews to cross the Red Sea. But God interrupted natural law and drew back the water so the people could cross safely on dry ground. Through an impossible situation, God was teaching the Hebrews a lesson in faith and, at the same time, bringing glory to His name. Miracles always glorify God. If a person receives the glory for performing miracles, we know that God isn't in them.

When, Then, Do They Occur?

Two facts help sort through some of today's common misconceptions about miracles. First, they are rare. "If miracles were commonplace," observes former Surgeon General C. Everett Koop, "they would cease to be miracles."[1] Even during Bible times, miracles appeared in certain periods more than others—during the days of Moses, Elijah and Elisha, and Christ and the apostles. Apart from these periods, God seldom interrupted the natural laws that govern His world.

Second, when miracles do occur, they are immediate. There's no waiting period for them to take full effect. Peter commanded the lame man to walk, seized his hand, and pulled him up from his mat. "*Immediately* his feet and his ankles were strengthened" (Acts 3:7, emphasis added). In an instant, atrophied muscles grew; severed tendons connected. He was leaping and walking and praising God.[2] And all the other biblical miracles follow this pattern.[3]

A Study of the Meal Christ Provided

In our passage, we find a miracle that was also a teachable moment on the subject of impossibilities. It's the extraordinary story of Christ feeding the multitudes.

---

1. C. Everett Koop, "Faith-Healing and the Sovereignty of God," in *The Agony of Deceit,* ed. Michael Horton (Chicago, Ill.: Moody Press, 1990), p. 175.

2. Healings such as these served as signs that validated a heavenly message. Unfortunately, people were often so mesmerized by the miracles, they ignored the message. "Forget the preaching, give us signs!" they clamored. But Jesus refused to play to the crowd. He condemned His generation because they sought after signs instead of truth (see Luke 11:29). But He is pleased when we take Him at His Word and walk a reasonable life of faith, doing what He has said to do.

3. For more examples, see Matthew 8:3; Luke 4:38–39; 8:44, 55.

The Setting

The disciples had just returned from their first attempts at ministry. Jesus had given them the power and authority to preach the gospel of the kingdom and heal diseases in His name. They had gone to every village in the area, and now this brood of faithlings had gathered back to Jesus, physically and emotionally worn out. Knowing they were exhausted, Jesus arranged an opportunity for them to get away from the crowds. "Taking them with Him, He withdrew by Himself to a city called Bethsaida" (Luke 9:10).

Imagine stretching out on a grassy mountainside overlooking a peaceful lake, relaxing beside the Lord who sprinkled the stars and swirled the galaxies. The disciples had just begun to unwind in this incredible setting of creation and Creator, when the atmosphere suddenly changed. Luke tells us that "the multitudes were aware of this and followed Him" (v. 11a).

People rowed across the sea, hiked over the hills, appeared from everywhere. The disciples wanted to be alone with the Lord, and here came an enormous crowd. According to verse 14, the number was about five thousand, not counting women and children. Graciously, though, the Lord welcomed them, "speaking to them about the kingdom of God and curing those who had need of healing" (v. 11b).

Into the afternoon Jesus fed the people from the overflowing storehouse of His grace, until, finally, "the day began to decline" (v. 12a). Spiritually, the people were satisfied. But physically, it was dinnertime, and they were hungry.

The disciples weren't sure what to do. Here they were in a barren place that no caterer would come near, with no food stores in sight, and thousands of stomachs growling expectantly. It was an impossible situation.

The Dialogue

And that's just how Jesus wanted it. John tells us that Jesus "knew what He was intending to do" (John 6:6). He was planning a miracle. Yet He didn't want to rush the miracle and miss the teachable moment.

As one group, His disciples came forward with worry written all over their faces.

> "Send the multitude away, that they may go into the surrounding villages and countryside and find

lodging and get something to eat; for here we are in
a desolate place." (Luke 9:12b)

Literally, the last phrase reads, "because here in a desolate place
we are." Weary and hungry, the disciples' eyes were on themselves
and their circumstances. Had they forgotten that in their midst was
the Creator who had brought forth the earth out of nothing? Ap-
parently so.

Jesus decided to press the disciples, giving them the chance to
admit their insufficiency and turn to Him in faith.

> But He said to them, "You give them something to
> eat!" And they said, "We have no more than five
> loaves and two fish, unless perhaps we go and buy
> food for all these people." (For there were about five
> thousand men.) (vv. 13–14a)

Jesus was joking, right? A nervous chuckle coursed through the
group. But Jesus was serious. According to John's account, Philip
pulled out a calculator and tried to help Him see the facts.

> Philip answered Him, "Two hundred denarii worth
> of bread is not sufficient for them, for everyone to
> receive a little." (John 6:7)

They didn't have that kind of money—that was nearly a year's
earnings. And even if they did, where could they buy the food?
The only food around was a little boy's sack lunch, which consisted
of five barley loaves and two fish (vv. 8–9). Jesus was asking the
impossible.

The Miracle

In the curriculum of faith, the subject of impossibilities was still
a grade level above the disciples' comprehension. So the Lord used
an object lesson to get His point across. In a quiet, unobtrusive
fashion, Jesus rang the bell for school to begin by having the disciples tell the people to sit down in groups of fifty and recline
(Luke 9:14–15). In other words, get ready to eat.

> And He took the five loaves and the two fish, and
> looking up to heaven, He blessed them, and broke
> them, and kept giving them to the disciples to set
> before the multitude. (v. 16)

You can't fully appreciate this unless you understand that these were most likely little pickled fish, like sardines, not great big bass or salmon. And barley loaves were the size of large pancakes—flat, hard, and brittle.

Jesus took these brittle loaves and tiny fish in His hands and pulled off the impossible. And who were the ones at hand, watching Him do it? Not the multitudes. They were seated too far away to see what was really going on. Only the disciples, Jesus' front-row students, witnessed the miracle clearly. Jesus got them personally involved in carrying it out too. He had said, "You give them something to eat." They had responded, "It can't be done." But now *they* were doing it!

The Results

> And they all ate and were satisfied; and the broken pieces which they had left over were picked up, twelve baskets full. (v. 17)

The disciples had reached the end of their resources. But Jesus multiplied what little they had, and the multitudes were satisfied. With each disciple bringing an overflowing basket of leftovers back to Jesus, they carried a reminder that, with Christ, all things are possible.

An Understanding of What This Means

Does an impossibility have you cornered? When asked to describe your situation, do words like *crisis, catastrophe,* or *disaster* come to mind, rather than *teachable moment?* If that's you, try looking at your circumstances through the lens of Luke's story, and keep in mind these three principles.

First, *when we are exhausted, we tend to think mainly of ourselves.* Weariness blurs our vision of God's plan. People's normal demands overwhelm us. We feel irritated, angry, depleted. But that's OK. Having run out of resources, we're now able to completely rely on the sufficiency of Christ.

Second, *when we are pressed, we tend to focus on what cannot be done.* None of the disciples thought about asking Jesus to perform a miracle—something He had been doing all day. They could see the size of the problem with clarity, but they couldn't see the size of God. Pressure makes pessimists of us all. Understanding this tendency can help us guard against it.

Third, *when we are rebuked, we tend to miss the insights God wants us to learn.* The disciples had to repeat the course of Faith 101 several times. Right after this episode, Mark says they panicked when they saw Jesus walking on water in a storm. The reason? "They had not gained any insight from the incident of the loaves, but their heart was hardened" (Mark 6:52).

When Jesus does the impossible in your life, open your heart. Miracles are too valuable to leave behind. Gather the memories into a basket, and keep them with you always.

 Living Insights

Sometimes when Jesus asks us to tackle a big job with little resources, we shake our heads in disbelief. We scan the five-thousand-plus crowd of hungry people and laugh. There might as well be twenty thousand; we barely have enough to feed one. How can Jesus ask us to give them something to eat? In desperation, we respond like Andrew—the disciple who brought forward the little boy with his loaves and fishes—"What are these for so many people?" (John 6:9).

That's a good question. It's the same question a single parent asks. There's only so much time and so much energy and so much wisdom to go around: "What are these for the needs of my family?"

It's the question asked by a new minister, who has just graduated from seminary with a sack lunch of experience and know-how. "What are these to feed a congregation of starving people?"

Are you asking that question too? Describe the task, then phrase the question to apply to your situation.

_____

_____

_____

_____

Sometimes we wonder, "Does the Lord realize what He's asking?" Yes, He does. He's counted the inventory in our warehouse. He's worked the numbers. He's calculated the odds. And He still says, "You give them something to eat!"

However, He doesn't intend for us to do the impossible on our own. He's there to multiply our meager resources when we give them to Him in faith and step out to serve.

Have you been holding on to your sackful of abilities, depending on them to get you through? Or, in frustration, have you simply stopped trying?

_____

_____

_____

How does the story of Jesus' multiplying the loaves and fish give you hope?

_____

_____

_____

Living Insights STUDY TWO

Some people think that if Jesus would just perform a miracle in their lives, they would believe in Him. But it's not wise to build a house of faith upon the shifting foundation of miracles. The reason is, one miracle is never enough. And neither are two or three or a dozen. We're always left wondering, "Will He do it again?"

That's what happened to the disciples. The multiplying of the loaves and fishes was spectacular, but when the food was eaten and the crowds left, so did the faith-inspiring impact of the miracle. Soon after, during a storm on the sea, the disciples quaked in fear. Mark says, "They had not gained any insight from the incident of the loaves" (Mark 6:52). Their walls crumbled.

God never intended miracles to support the full weight of our faith. Then what does He want us to build our lives upon? Turn back and read Luke 6:47–49 for the answer.

_____

_____

On what have you built your faith?

_____

_____

_____

Is this a solid foundation? What do you need to do to shore it up?

_____

_____

_____

Don't build your faith on miracles. Build it on Christ. The miracles may come; they may not. But Christ's presence will endure.

Chapter 11

A SHOCKING AGENDA

Luke 9:18–27

Living under the boot of Roman domination, the Jews longed for their Deliverer—the descendant of David who would lift them out of the mud and set them on top of the world. Centuries earlier, Isaiah painted a portrait of this coming Savior:

> For a child will be born to us, a son will be given
>   to us;
> And the government will rest on His shoulders;
> And His name will be called Wonderful Counselor,
>   Mighty God,
> Eternal Father, Prince of Peace.
> There will be no end to the increase of His
>   government or of peace,
> On the throne of David and over his kingdom,
> To establish it and to uphold it with justice and
>   righteousness
> From then on and forevermore. (Isa. 9:6–7)

Prophecies like this one filled the people's hearts with dreams of an eternal kingdom of peace, justice, and righteousness. Think of it! No more oppression. No more fear. No more taxes! During Jesus' day, messianic hopes coursed through the tiny nation of Palestine like an electric current. Michael Green, in his book *Who Is This Jesus?*, writes,

> Everyone was on tiptoe of expectation that the *kingdom of God* would soon break in. Things were very dark, but then, the darkest hour always comes before the dawn.[1]

For months, Jesus had been radiating kingdom light into the world's darkness. He had preached kingdom truth, displayed kingdom power, and modeled kingdom righteousness. The disciples naturally expected Jesus to unveil the dawn's full and dazzling light

---

1. Michael Green, *Who Is This Jesus?* (Nashville, Tenn.: Thomas Nelson Publishers, Oliver Nelson, 1992), p. 19.

at any moment. However, Jesus had another plan in mind, an agenda that would shock even His closest friends.

The Question Each Person Must Answer

Disclosing His agenda was a critical turning point in Jesus' life, one that He wanted to approach prayerfully. Luke says that He "was praying alone" (Luke 9:18a), as He often did at significant moments: His baptism (3:21), the selection of the disciples (6:12–13), and later, at Gethsemane (22:39–46).[2]

Perhaps, in His prayers, the recent weeks of whirlwind ministry blew across His mind. Had anyone understood the message He had been laboring to communicate? So He turned toward His disciples, who Luke says "were with Him" (9:18a), and asked,

"Who do the multitudes say that I am?" (v. 18b)

Having mingled among the people, the Twelve had heard all the rumors.

And they answered and said, "John the Baptist, and others say Elijah; but others, that one of the prophets of old has risen again." (v. 19)

Then Jesus brought the issue to a deeply personal level, probing the disciples' hearts with a question that every person in every generation must answer:

"But who do you say that I am?" (v. 20a)

How would you answer that question? Some people say that He was a good man who taught peace and harmony. Or that He was a wise leader who got caught in the crossfire between politics and religion. Peter, however, gave the true response—He is "the Christ of God" (v. 20b).

Jesus is *the Christ*—literally, "the anointed One," the Messiah. And He is *of God*; He is deity. He is the One of whom the prophets spoke. He is the fulfillment of our dreams. The Wonderful Coun-selor. The Mighty God. The Eternal Father. The Prince of Peace.

---

2. Jesus never pressured His disciples to pray like Him; He simply prayed and they watched Him. They observed prayer's impact in His life and, like children, longed to follow in His footsteps (see Luke 11:1).

The disciples yearned to shout it from the mountaintops, but Jesus clapped His hand over their mouths:

> But He warned them, and instructed them not to tell this to anyone. (v. 21)

How puzzling. Why would the King silence the trumpets announcing His presence? Why would He tell His chief spokesmen to be quiet about the news that all Jews were longing to hear?

One reason could have been that He didn't want to start a revolution. Overthrowing Roman authority was not His plan; His objective went far beyond an earthly revolt. Another possible reason was that, in His day, one didn't claim messiahship for oneself; others were to observe and declare the truth of it. Either way, His guarded response was preparing the disciples for a disturbing look into the future.

The Plan Each Disciple Had to Accept

Jesus was indeed the Messiah. But not the conquering political hero the disciples had imagined. Gravely, He announced,

> "The Son of Man must suffer many things, and be rejected by the elders and chief priests and scribes, and be killed, and be raised up on the third day." (v. 22)

Look at the verbs: *suffer, be rejected, be killed, be raised.* These words must have hit the disciples like four punches to the stomach. Matthew, in his gospel, records that Peter responded with a desperate rebuke: "God forbid it, Lord! This shall never happen to You" (Matt. 16:22). Peter didn't understand—none of the disciples did. Later, Jesus tried again to help them see the truth. "Let these words sink into your ears," He pleaded.

> "For the Son of Man is going to be delivered into the hands of men." But they did not understand this statement. (Luke 9:44–45a)

They couldn't fathom the mysteries of the redemption that Jesus' death would provide. All they heard was that the Messiah—who they thought had come to rescue the nation—was going to die. It didn't make sense to them. But Jesus had even more difficult statements to deliver.

91

The Commands Each Christian Should Obey

Implicit in Jesus' earlier question, "Who do you say that I am?" is another, more penetrating question, "What difference does it make to you?" Having clarified Peter's answer to the first question—that He will be a suffering Messiah—Jesus next reveals what's involved in the answer to that second question.

> And He was saying to them all, "If anyone wishes
> to come after Me, let him deny himself, and take
> up his cross daily, and follow Me." (v. 23)

That *all* includes us today who, having trusted Christ for salvation, desire to be His disciples. Jesus could have opened a file cabinet of requirements for us: "If people wish to come after Me, they must have a strong work ethic, a winsome personality, and an IQ of at least 150. Of course, they must be educated—no dropouts, please. They must be attractive, have good table manners. . . ." No, Christ has only three requirements.

Disciples Must Deny Themselves

Some Christians have erroneously taken this to mean that they must cultivate a mousy, self-effacing personality or that they should deny themselves of pleasures and preferences in life. They make a mental list of the things they enjoy, from eating chocolate to reading good novels, and abstain from them in the name of self-denial.

But that's not what Jesus is talking about. He's saying that if we want to follow Him, we must put His will above our own. We must recognize His right to rule over our lives. If He says, "Do that," or, "Don't do that," we comply, even when our nature cries out for us to do the opposite. Self-denial essentially means obedience.

Disciples Must Take Up Their Crosses Daily

In Jesus' day, a condemned criminal was forced to carry the crossbeam upon which he would be hung at his own crucifixion. When people saw someone struggling under that piece of timber, they knew they'd never see that person return. He was on a journey of death.

Likewise, those who wish to be Jesus' disciples must die to self-centeredness and self-absorption. And because selfishness doesn't ever seem to die a once-for-all death, we must execute it daily.

For example, we need to die to the plans and dreams that do

not align with God's plans and dreams for us. To be painfully specific, is it God's plan for us to amass and cling to transitory material possessions we really can't afford? Or would He have us invest our energy in what lasts—the well-being of our marriages and emotional health of our children? Is our dream of finding deepest intimacy outside of marriage God's dream for us?

Our ways can lead to harm (see Prov. 14:12), but God's ways always lead to true life.[3]

Disciples Must Follow Him

Today's philosophers tell us we must follow ourselves. "Your journey is within," they say. They teach us to worship at the shrine of "I, me, mine, myself," to measure relationships only by how well they help us blossom as individuals, to look out only for number one.

However, living only for ourselves is an inwardly spiraling journey that leads nowhere. Sadly, those who follow this path lose the very thing they worked so hard to gain—a reason for living. Only by following Jesus' example of love, self-sacrifice, and intimacy with the Father do we discover who we are and why we are here. Jesus put it this way:

> "For whoever wishes to save his life shall lose it, but whoever loses his life for My sake, he is the one who will save it." (Luke 9:24)

No doubt, living selfishly may reap rich earthly rewards. But, as Jesus asked, is wealth worth the price of a human soul?

> "For what is a man profited if he gains the whole world, and loses or forfeits himself? For whoever is ashamed of Me and My words, of him will the Son of Man be ashamed when He comes in His glory, and the glory of the Father and of the holy angels." (vv. 25–26)

Jim Elliot, one of five missionaries who died attempting to reach the Huaorani (Auca) Indians with the gospel, exemplified these principles. His words echo clearly the teaching of Jesus:

---

3. William Barclay presents a more literal view: "To take up our cross means to be prepared to face things like [crucifixion] for loyalty to Jesus; it means to be ready to endure the worst that man can do to us for the sake of being true to him." *The Gospel of Luke*, rev. ed., The Daily Study Bible Series (Philadelphia, Pa.: Westminster Press, 1975), p. 121.

He is no fool who gives what he cannot keep to gain
what he cannot lose.[4]

To follow Christ, the wise person willingly gives up the glass
baubles of this world in exchange for the diamonds of God's kingdom. Yet how difficult it is to wait. We are, by nature, like children
with a pocketful of money, eager to buy glitzy, plastic trinkets now
rather than save up for something of lasting value. We need a power
beyond us to help us discern and go toward what really matters and
leave the rest behind, which is what Christ may very well have
intimated in verse 27:

> "But I say to you truthfully, there are some of those
> standing here who shall not taste death until they
> see the kingdom of God."

Christ may have been referring to the Day of Pentecost, when
all of the disciples except Judas would receive God's kingdom power
when the Holy Spirit came upon them (see Acts 1:8; 2:1–4; see
also Mark 9:1).[5] At that time, with the Spirit's power, they would
finally taste the "death" of dying to their own will and living for Christ.

The Issues Each of Us Has to Face

What does it mean for us to live for Christ's kingdom today?
First, *following Christ means more than believing Him—it includes
obedience*. By believing in Christ, we receive His gift of eternal life;
by obeying Him, we become His disciples and are transformed in
our daily life.

Second, *living obediently means more than accepting the truth—it
includes "tasting death."* That is, it includes putting to death our
selfish desires in favor of Christ's will for our lives.

Third, *tasting death means more than being unselfish—it includes
dying daily*. Pride bellows, "I want what I want when I want it!"
Listening to its voice, we push for our rights and demand our way.
We surround ourselves with good people who applaud our "courage."

4. Jim Elliot, as quoted by Elisabeth Elliot in *Shadow of the Almighty: The Life and Testament
of Jim Elliot* (Grand Rapids, Mich.: Zondervan Publishing House, 1958), p. 15.

5. Some commentators believe that Christ was referring to the Transfiguration in the phrase
"until they see the kingdom of God." For a discussion of this and other interpretations of
Luke 9:27, see *The Bible Knowledge Commentary*, New Testament edition, ed. John F. Walvoord
and Roy B. Zuck (Wheaton, Ill.: Scripture Press Publications, Victor Books, 1983), pp. 142, 230.

But through the noise, Jesus' words continue to ring: "Whoever loses his life for My sake, he is the one who will save it."

He lays the choice before us. Will we say no to our own agendas? Will we daily crucify the idols of self-worship? Will we follow Him?

 Living Insights

Some of the sayings of Scripture, like the Proverbs, are pebbles of truth that we can easily pick up and slip into our pockets. Jesus' sayings in this passage are like huge boulders. To move them into our lives, we must chip off little bits of understanding here and there as we are able.

The late V. Raymond Edman—author, college president, missionary—provided us with a nugget of insight by his own example. From his testimony, we can grasp a little of what it means to deny ourselves, take up our crosses, and follow Jesus:

> I had utterly abandoned myself to Him. . . . Could any choice be as wonderful as His will? Could any place be safer than the center of His will? Did not He assure me by His very Presence that His thoughts toward us are good, and not evil? Death to my own plans and desires was almost deliriously delightful. Everything was laid at His nail-scarred feet, life or death, health or illness, appreciation by others or misunderstanding, success or failure as measured by human standards. Only He Himself mattered.[6]

Can you relate to his testimony? What new understanding of Christ's words can you move into your life as a result of our study?

_____

_____

_____

_____

6. V. Raymond Edman, as quoted in *World Shapers: A Treasury of Quotes from Great Missionaries,* comp. Vinita Hampton and Carol Plueddemann (Wheaton, Ill.: Harold Shaw Publishers, 1991), p. 17.

 *Living Insights*

Between 1969 and 1973, Chuck Colson had gained the world. He was special counsel to President Nixon and perhaps the most powerful attorney in America. Then the Watergate scandal shook the White House, and his carefully constructed life collapsed in a heap. He was tried, convicted, and behind bars within a year.

Just prior to his conviction, however, Colson had given his life to Christ. God would use prison, Colson's lowest point, as a turning point in his life. Because of what he saw in prison, Colson would later form Prison Fellowship, a ministry to inmates around the world.

Colson's testimony reminds us of the marvelous paradox of Jesus' words: "For what is a man profited if he gains the whole world, and loses or forfeits himself?" (Luke 9:25). Read what this verse means to him as he reflects on how God is using his life to impact thousands of hardened prisoners.

> All my achievements meant nothing in God's econ-omy. No, the real legacy of my life was my biggest failure—that I was an ex-convict. My greatest humiliation—being sent to prison—was the begin-ning of God's greatest use of my life; He chose the one experience in which I could not glory for *His* glory.
>
> Confronted with this staggering truth, I dis-covered . . . that my world was turned upside down. I understood with a jolt that I had been looking at life backward. But now I could see: only when I lost everything I thought made Chuck Colson a great guy had I found the true self God intended me to be and the true purpose of my life.
>
> It is not what we do that matters, *but what a sovereign God chooses to do through us.* God doesn't want our success; He wants us. He doesn't demand our achievements; He demands our obedience.[7]

Have you found the "true self" God intended you to be? Has your striving to "gain the world" blurred your vision of who you are

---

7. Charles W. Colson, *Loving God* (Grand Rapids, Mich.: Zondervan Publishing House, 1987), pp. 24–25.

and your true purpose for living? As Colson writes, God doesn't want your success; He wants you. He doesn't demand your achievements; He demands your obedience.

We've provided you some space to work out exactly what that means for you. Has Christ brought you to a turning point? Do you need to make some important decisions about your life's direction? What do you need to lose in order to save your life? Before you write, take some time to listen to His voice helping you know what you should do.

_____

_____

_____

_____

_____

_____

_____

_____

_____

_____

_____

_____

_____

_____

_____

_____

Chapter 12

THE ULTIMATE CLOSE ENCOUNTER

Luke 9:28–36

Many of us view supernatural encounters with the skeptical eye of Ebenezer Scrooge. Charles Dickens, in his classic *A Christmas Carol*, describes Scrooge's eerie visit with the very dead Jacob Marley:

> "You don't believe in me," observed the Ghost.
> "I don't." said Scrooge.
> "What evidence would you have of my reality beyond that of your senses?"
> "I don't know," said Scrooge.
> "Why do you doubt your senses?"
> "Because," said Scrooge, "a little thing affects them. A slight disorder of the stomach makes them cheats. You may be an undigested bit of beef, a blot of mustard, a crumb of cheese, a fragment of an underdone potato. There's more of gravy than of grave about you, whatever you are!"[1]

Like Scrooge, we tend to reach for natural explanations of supernatural events. We hear stories about angelic visitations, and our first response is, "Humbug. A bit of beef, that's all." Perhaps our skepticism is the by-product of our tabloid diet of visits with vampires and alien abductions. Certainly, there's much worth doubting in our world, but, if taken sensibly, there is also much worth believing.

A Few Sensible Remarks about the Supernatural

What do we know about the supernatural? First, *though we cannot prove it, we know the supernatural exists*. Although we can't study the spirit world under a laboratory microscope, we can see glimpses

---

1. Charles Dickens, *A Christmas Carol*, in *A Treasury of Christmas Classics* (Wheaton, Ill.: Harold Shaw Publishers, 1994), pp. 60–61.

of it through the telescope of Scripture. The writer to the Hebrews indicates that we could encounter an angel at any time.

> Do not neglect to show hospitality to strangers, for by this some have entertained angels without knowing it. (13:2)

Daniel provides us with a fascinating look at spiritual warfare in chapter 10 of his book. A powerful demon, "the prince of the kingdom of Persia," delays an angelic messenger from answering Daniel's prayer, until the mighty angel Michael battles the demon so the messenger can make it through (Dan. 10:1–13). If only our eyes were opened, like the eyes of Elisha's servant, we would be amazed at the throng of supernatural forces around us all the time (see 2 Kings 6:15–17).

Second, *though we cannot understand it, we believe in the supernatural.* Our hope of eternal life rests in our belief in a world beyond our own where God has established His glorious throne, angels worship Him, and Jesus sits at His right hand, interceding on our behalf and preparing a place for us (see Rom. 8:34; John 14:2). Paul calls this place "the third heaven" and "Paradise" (2 Cor. 12:2, 4). We may not be able to see or feel it, but as sure as God's Word is true, it's real.

Third, *though we may not have experienced it, we acknowledge that others have.* We've heard many stories of supernatural encounters told by reliable sources: the dying person who sees angels standing nearby; the resuscitated person who tells of stepping into a magnificent light, only to be pulled back into this life; the missionaries who encounter demons in non-Christian cultures. Few of these people sought out the supernatural or were prone to embroider the truth, yet they report brushes with the spirit world that defy natural explanation. These reports are surely too frequent and the details too consistent to be ignored.

Old Scrooge, of course, would have humbugged their stories— as he would have humbugged the extraordinary event that Luke records in our passage. But if we can believe in supernatural things we don't understand, than we can believe that this event occurred just as Luke said it did.

Some Careful Observations of the Transfiguration

Luke wasn't the only one to chronicle this event; Matthew and

Mark recorded it also, and all of them with striking similarity (compare Matt. 17:1–8; Mark 9:2–8). It is known as the Transfiguration—the amazing moment when Jesus metamorphosed into His heavenly form. Let's examine this phenomenal event through the lenses of four questions: who, what, how, and why.

Who Was There?

Not all the disciples witnessed the Transfiguration. Jesus selected only three to come with Him, the same three who saw Him bring to life Jairus' daughter (Luke 8:41–51).

> And some eight days after these sayings, it came about that He took along Peter and John and James, and went up to the mountain to pray. (9:28)

About a week earlier, Jesus had dropped the bombshell that He would die and be raised on the third day (v. 22).[2] We're not told what took place during that week. Maybe the disciples finally found the needed opportunity to have Jesus all to themselves and to ponder the scope of His high calling. Whatever happened, it was a down time for the ministry. A time to relax. And a time, perhaps, for fear about the future to gain a foothold in the disciples' hearts. For whatever reason, Jesus whispered to Peter, John, and James, "Let's go find a quiet place to pray."

Four men scaled that high mountain, but two more men would appear out of nowhere—two who had been dead for more than a thousand years. This is where the story gets supernatural.

What Occurred?

> And while He was praying, the appearance of His face became different, and His clothing became white and gleaming. And behold, two men were talking with Him; and they were Moses and Elijah, who, appearing in glory, were speaking of His departure which He was about to accomplish at Jerusalem. (vv. 29–31)

Luke's word for *gleaming* literally means "to flash forth as

---

2. Matthew and Mark say "six days" instead of Luke's "eight days." Luke was probably including the day Jesus made His announcement and the day of His transfiguration, while Matthew and Mark were only counting the days in between.

lightning."[3] Matthew says that "His face shone like the sun, and His garments became as white as light" (Matt. 17:2). Mark reports that "His garments became radiant and exceedingly white, as no launderer on earth can whiten them" (Mark 9:3).

The veil of humanity had been drawn back, revealing Jesus' divine glory—the same Shechinah glory that lit Mount Sinai with its "consuming fire" (Exod. 24:17) . . . the same glory that preceded Israel through the wilderness and filled the Tabernacle (Exod. 40:34–38) . . . the same glory that would stun Saul on the road to Damascus and change His life forever (Acts 9:3–8).

Appearing also in "glory" were Moses and Elijah. Having come straight from the presence of God, they bore the reflection of His splendor. Moses represented the Law; and Elijah, the Prophets—writings that Jesus had come to fulfill (Luke 24:44). And now, in this historic moment, the Old Testament was meeting its Messiah.

Luke says they "were speaking of His departure which He was about to accomplish at Jerusalem" (9:31). Both Moses and Elijah had departed from this life in divinely appointed ways—Moses died on Mount Nebo and was buried by God Himself (Deut. 34:1–6); Elijah was taken up to heaven in the whirlwind of a fiery chariot (2 Kings 2:11). And Jesus' death was divinely arranged as well. It would be the culmination of God's redemptive plan of the ages. Unlike the disciples, though, Moses and Elijah understood this plan perfectly, and they had come to encourage Jesus to keep going until He had fulfilled all of what was predicted.

How Did the Disciples Respond?

At first, Peter, John, and James were unaware of what was happening, for they "had been overcome with sleep" (Luke 9:32a). Perhaps the long climb had worn them out, and the rare moment of quiet and the beautiful setting had lulled them to sleep. In any event, Luke makes sure to say that they weren't dreaming now.

> When they were fully awake, they saw His glory and
> the two men standing with Him. (v. 32b)

Mark adds that "they became terrified" (Mark 9:6). Witnessing God's glory always makes the most courageous quail. Experiencing

---

3. Fritz Rienecker, *A Linguistic Key to the Greek New Testament*, ed. Cleon Rogers, Jr. (Grand Rapids, Mich.: Zondervan Publishing House, Regency Reference Library, 1980), p. 166.

the ultimate supernatural close encounter, these men felt their legs turn to rubber. Only Peter had the nerve, or perhaps the foolishness, to speak.

> And it came about, as these were parting from Him, Peter said to Jesus, "Master, it is good for us to be here; and let us make three tabernacles: one for You, and one for Moses, and one for Elijah"—not realizing what he was saying. (Luke 9:33)

Peter's words bolted from his heart and stampeded out of his mouth before his mind had a chance to corral them. He wanted to build some tents so that Moses and Elijah could stay longer. He forgot that supernatural beings didn't need a covering over their heads.[4] He also forgot that God was in charge of the situation, a fact that God quickly made clear to everyone:

> And while he was saying this, a cloud formed and began to overshadow them; and they were afraid as they entered the cloud. (v. 34)

Like the foreboding cloud that enshrouded Mount Sinai, God's presence came upon them like a dense fog. At once, the disciples were cut off. They couldn't see two inches in front of their faces, but what they heard was unmistakable.

> And a voice came out of the cloud, saying, "This is My Son, My Chosen One; listen to Him!" (v. 35)

Matthew writes that, at the sound of these words, "they fell on their faces," overwhelmed with fear (Matt. 17:6). Then, as quickly as it had all happened, it was gone, and God's Chosen One stood alone before the disciples. The sun resumed its role as the brightest light in the sky. The encounter was over. The disciples would never forget what they saw, but for the time being

> they kept silent, and reported to no one in those days any of the things which they had seen. (Luke 9:36)

---

4. Commentator John A. Martin adds this insight into Peter's response: the disciples "realized they were in a kingdom setting which triggered Peter's idea that they build three shelters. Peter may have been thinking of the Feast of Booths, a feast of ingathering long associated with the coming kingdom (cf. Zech. 14:16–21). Peter seemed to have assumed that the kingdom had arrived." See "Luke," in *The Bible Knowledge Commentary*, New Testament edition, ed. John F. Walvoord and Roy B. Zuck (Wheaton, Ill.: Scripture Press Publications, Victor Books, 1983), p. 231.

They kept silent . . . until another supernatural event occurred: the Resurrection. Then they told the world the incredible story of what had happened that day (see 2 Pet. 1:16–18).

Why Did It Happen?

There's always a reason for a heavenly encounter, and the Transfiguration probably served two purposes. First, Moses and Elijah came to reassure Jesus to keep pushing ahead, all the way to the Cross. And second, God spoke to the disciples to remind them that Jesus was the Chosen One. Perhaps doubts about His identity had crept into their hearts. Maybe they weren't sure they wanted to deny themselves, take up their crosses, and follow Him. God used this experience to put steel into their commitment.

Two Enduring Principles from the Story

In the lingering light of the Transfiguration story, we see two lasting principles. First, *pursuing God's plan is always best, though it may include pain, suffering, and even death.* We get cold feet sometimes in our desire to pursue God's plan. Jesus encourages us as Moses and Elijah encouraged Him: "Stay with God's plan. Although painful now, in the end, it will turn out for good."

Second, *following God's Son is always best, since no one else qualifies as God's Chosen One.* If Peter, John, and James wondered whether Jesus was truly the Messiah, their doubts dissipated that day on the mountain. Do you ever wonder whether Jesus is the only way? Whether His words are truth? Whether following Him really leads to life? Picture Him as the disciples saw Him, appearing in glory, outshining the sun. He truly is the Son of God.

 Living Insights STUDY ONE

When times are hard, doubts hail and storm in your soul, making your faith grow cold. How warming it would be if the Lord would reveal Himself to you. It doesn't need to be spectacular. Just a small revelation. Something. Anything.

As much as we long for them, however, supernatural manifestations are not a cure-all. Remember what happened to Peter during Jesus' trials? He had witnessed Christ perform hundreds of miracles, including His incredible Transfiguration. If glimpses of the supernatural strengthen faith, Peter's should have been ironclad. Yet, when he denied the Lord three times, his faith folded like a house of cards (see Luke 22:54–62).

What gives our faith staying power? God's Word. Christ drew encouragement from Moses and Elijah, representatives of the Law and the Prophets. Where do you go in the Scriptures to strengthen your faith? One prophet, Isaiah, has some encouragement to share with you. Pick out a faith-building truth from each reference to sustain you in the days ahead.

30:18–22 _____

_____

33:2–6 _____

_____

43:16–21 _____

_____

50:8–10 _____

_____

 Living Insights   STUDY TWO

Artists around the world have painted Jesus in all the colors of the cultural rainbow. The African Christ is mahogany-skinned with dark hair and full lips. The Korean Christ has almond eyes and penciled brows. The Russian Christ has a furrowed forehead and narrow eyes. The American Christ has brown eyes, flowing hair, and a sculptured nose.

It is good that each culture can imagine Him as their own. After all, He is a Savior for the world.

He invites us to see Him in our own image, to call Him *our* Lord. But we must never forget to also see Him as He is, the glorious Son of God. In every culture, the transfigured Christ remains the same.

So far, Luke has revealed Jesus as one of us. Very human. Very touchable. Now, in the resplendent light of the Transfiguration, Luke shows Christ as separate. We can worship but we cannot cling to this Jesus.

How do you see Jesus? Does Luke's account of His Transfiguration provide an added dimension to your understanding of Christ? In what ways?

_____

_____

_____

_____

Identifying with you in your weaknesses, the human Jesus provides you comfort. In what ways can you draw comfort from the divine Jesus who rises above your frailties?

_____

_____

_____

_____

The world has as many ideas about Jesus as paintings of Him. Don't get lost in the gallery of opinions. Keep your worship focused on the transfigured Christ, and you'll always find your way to the truth.

Chapter 13

SNAPSHOTS FROM AN AMAZING ALBUM

Luke 9:37–62

A piercing tone knifes through the darkness, stabbing you awake. The smoke detector! In a split second, you throw aside the covers and sprint toward the children's rooms. Frantically, you shake the sleepy bodies, gather everyone together, and stumble through the stinging smoke to the front door. As the family scrambles to safety, your mind races. If you hurry, you have just enough time to save one thing from the fire—your most valuable belonging. What would it be?

Many people would run for the family photo albums because they hold irreplaceable memories: a grandmother cuddling the first grandchild, a favorite uncle who died last year, the silly skit the kids put on for the family. These photos are more than glossy images on paper; they give meaning and history to our lives.

The gospels are like those family albums. They contain precious pictures of Jesus, taken at different times and from different perspectives. Having carefully laid out these images, the gospel writers invite us to pore over them so we can take His life into ours. In this next section of Luke, we'll reflect on images from five scenes in Jesus' life—scenes that make Luke's gospel one of our most valuable possessions.

A Photographic Journey through a Part of Jesus' Ministry

Luke's images resemble what we might find on a roll of film in our own cameras—a shot or two left over from vacation, a series of birthday shots taken later on, a few holiday photos taken three months down the road. In the first set of shots in Luke 9:37–43a, he portrays what happened the day after the Transfiguration. No sooner had Jesus, Peter, John, and James returned from their mountaintop experience than the heartrending realities of ministry were upon them.

A Demonized Victim

And it came about on the next day, that when

they had come down from the mountain, a great multitude met Him. And behold, a man from the multitude shouted out, saying, "Teacher, I beg You to look at my son, for he is my only boy, and behold, a spirit seizes him, and he suddenly screams, and it throws him into a convulsion with foaming at the mouth, and as it mauls him, it scarcely leaves him. And I begged Your disciples to cast it out, and they could not." (Luke 9:37–40)

Luke compassionately captures the emotions in this scene: the pain of the desperate father, the pathetic condition of the child, the distress of the unsuccessful disciples. And he displays Jesus' feelings as well. The Lord's eyes betray a heart full of anguish over a world gone bad, where devils abuse innocent children and adults feel powerless to help. With a mixture of sadness and frustration, He, too, cries out:

"O unbelieving and perverted generation, how long shall I be with you, and put up with you?" (v. 41a)

Then, with deep empathy, He tells the father, "Bring your son here" (v. 41b). This is one battle the good guys are going to win.

And while he was still approaching, the demon dashed him to the ground, and threw him into a convulsion. But Jesus rebuked the unclean spirit, and healed the boy, and gave him back to his father.[1] (v. 42)

With tears of relief, father and son are reunited. The crowd marvels "at the greatness of God" (v. 43)—in Greek, "the *megaleiotēs* of God." It's a majestic word, meaning "splendor, magnificence."[2] Through the miracle, Jesus directs the people's praise where it should always go, to God.

The Stunned Disciples

Then, quietly, Luke turns the page of his photo album, and a

---

1. Some commentators would explain away the boy's affliction as the grand mal seizures of epilepsy. But the phrase "it mauls him" in verse 39 and Jesus' direct rebuke in verse 42 indicate that his condition went beyond a terrible physical disease to something worse.

2. See G. Abbott-Smith, *A Manual Greek Lexicon of the New Testament*, 3d ed. (Edinburgh, Scotland: T. and T. Clark, 1937), p. 281. Interestingly, *megaleiotēs* is the same word Peter uses to describe the majesty of Christ at His transfiguration (see 2 Pet. 1:16).

serious scene lies before us. In the midst of the rejoicing, Jesus leans over to remind the disciples that the marveling support will soon change to opposition.

> But while everyone was marveling at all that He was doing, He said to His disciples, "Let these words sink into your ears; for the Son of Man is going to be delivered into the hands of men." (vv. 43b–44)

Though He has told them this before (see v. 22), His declaration still stuns the disciples. According to Luke, "They did not understand this statement" (v. 45a). Instead of sinking in, Jesus' words seemed to shatter against a wall of preconceived ideas about His (and their) glorious future. Betrayal? Death at the hands of men? Jesus' popularity rating has never been higher. It doesn't make sense.

Also, perhaps to protect them from having to deal with more than they could bear,

> it was concealed from them so that they might not perceive it; and they were afraid to ask Him about this statement. (v. 45b; see also John 16:12–13)

A Child in Their Midst

The next scene takes place some time later. Luke pictures the disciples nose to nose in heated debate: "An argument arose among them as to which of them might be the greatest" (Luke 9:46). How quickly the praises for God's greatness have faded. Now the disciples are vying for highest honors among themselves. Jesus probably wished He could send them all to their rooms. Instead, He calls upon a child to help teach them a lesson about being an adult.

> But Jesus, knowing what they were thinking in their heart, took a child and stood him by His side, and said to them, "Whoever receives this child in My name receives Me; and whoever receives Me receives Him who sent Me; for he who is least among you, this is the one who is great." (vv. 47–48)

Traveling life's fast track to success, we tend to zoom past what God values most highly—the guileless, teachable spirit of a child. What a quiet but potent rebuke to the selfish, jealous, and competitive disciples . . . and to us. We need to stop galloping through life on our high horse, slow down, and dismount, for it is only when we take time to make room in our hearts for "the least of these" that we have the time and room for Jesus Himself (see also Matt. 25:31–46).

A Lesson on Tolerance

The scenes change quickly as John, perhaps embarrassed about the arguing, changes the subject.

> And John answered and said, "Master, we saw someone casting out demons in Your name; and we tried to hinder him because he does not follow along with us." (Luke 9:49)

Like good soldiers, the disciples have been protecting their Captain from competitors. Instead of a pat on the back, however, Jesus gives them a lesson on the difference between a friend and an enemy:

> But Jesus said to him, "Do not hinder him; for he who is not against you is for you."[3] (v. 50)

Sometimes loyal soldiers can do their leader harm by guarding him or her too closely. Unwittingly, when we stick by only one teacher or subscribe to only one ministry or denomination, we encourage a narrow, exclusive spirit. It's a dangerous thing to presume that God approves of no other work but ours. It fosters pride and pettiness. But Jesus models a humility that welcomes and encourages variety.

A Resolute Will

Luke's fifth scene opens with a dramatic portrait of Christ.

> And it came about, when the days were approaching for His ascension, that He resolutely set His face to go to Jerusalem. (v. 51)

Jesus has fixed His eyes on one purpose—the salvation of the world. Every step He takes now on His journey to Jerusalem is one step closer to the Cross. From here on, its shadow touches every conversation, every story, every moment. Not a day will pass that

---

3. See Numbers 11:24–30 for a similar scene between a loyal and protective Joshua and a greathearted Moses.

He does not envision that cruel timber upon which He will pour out His life for ours.

The book of Luke hinges on this verse, which marks the beginning of the last six months of Jesus' ministry. From here through chapter 21, the emphasis shifts from miracles to parables, from deeds to words (see the survey chart at the beginning of this study guide). The Son of God is crossing the bridge to Calvary, and there's no turning Him back.

Jesus looks for that same spirit of determination when it comes to our obedience. So Luke's next snapshots highlight four potential obstacles we must determine to overcome as we follow Him. The first focuses on rejection.

> And He sent messengers on ahead of Him. And they went, and entered a village of the Samaritans, to make arrangements for Him. And they did not receive Him, because He was journeying with His face toward Jerusalem. And when His disciples James and John saw this, they said, "Lord, do You want us to command fire to come down from heaven and consume them?" But He turned and rebuked them, and said, "You do not know what kind of spirit you are of; for the Son of Man did not come to destroy men's lives, but to save them." And they went on to another village. (9:52–56)

When the Cross is on our hearts as it was on Jesus' heart, giving life is more important than taking revenge. Jesus warns us not to get sidetracked by others' responses. Instead, press on!

Another obstacle to overcome is intimidation.

> And as they were going along the road, someone said to Him, "I will follow You wherever You go." And Jesus said to him, "The foxes have holes, and the birds of the air have nests, but the Son of Man has nowhere to lay His head." (vv. 57–58)

Jesus met the person's rash statement with a dose of harsh reality. He wasn't intimidated by others' zeal, and we shouldn't be either. Press on!

A third obstacle concerns distractions.

> And He said to another, "Follow Me." But he said,

"Permit me first to go and bury my father." But He said to him, "Allow the dead to bury their own dead; but as for you, go and proclaim everywhere the kingdom of God." (vv. 59–60)

For this person, the affairs of family are a higher priority than the affairs of Christ. The father may not even have been dead yet. The lesson: Don't get distracted by lesser loyalties. Press on!

Priorities are also an issue in the last obstacle.

And another also said, "I will follow You, Lord; but first permit me to say good-bye to those at home." But Jesus said to him, "No one, after putting his hand to the plow and looking back, is fit for the kingdom of God." (vv. 61–62)

Saying good-bye, for this person, may have been the first bead in a string of delays in following Jesus. From him we learn not to get misguided by a lower priority. Press on!

A Panoramic Summary of Jesus' Impact

Many more pictures await us in Luke's photo album, but let's pause before going further and pick out three principles from this collage of images.

First, *Christ expects our minds to be strong.* Satan yearns to control our lives like he did the demonized boy. He blinds the minds of the unbelieving (2 Cor. 4:4). He distorts the truth and distracts our focus. So we must let Christ's words sink into our souls—they will guard our minds against the attacks of the enemy and help us see God's will without distortion.

Second, *He desires that our hearts be soft.* He wants to cultivate in us the tender qualities of humility and innocence. He wants our attitude toward outsiders to be like His, tolerant and patient. These are the characteristics that lead to greatness in His eyes.

Third, *He is concerned that our wills be sure.* Have you resolutely set your will to follow Christ? Perhaps other pursuits have taken priority: finishing school, waiting for the dust to settle after a family crisis or a divorce, trying to get the business up and running. Jesus is saying—*now*—"Follow Me." Will you answer, "I will follow You, Lord, *but first* . . ."? Don't let those two words hinder you from accepting His call.

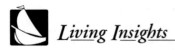

Living Insights

Mind. Heart. Will. These are the three battlefields of the soul. For a few moments, scan the war zones and give a report on the action.

First, review the battle for your mind. If the following statements are true for you, Satan could be gaining ground:

- I dwell on self-accusing thoughts like, "I'll never get it right" or "God could never forgive me."

- The world's me-first propaganda is starting to sound right.

- Rationalizing is becoming a habit.

Christ is getting the upper hand if these statements apply:

- I'm dwelling on "whatever is true, whatever is honorable, whatever is right, whatever is pure, whatever is lovely, whatever is of good repute, if there is any excellence and if anything worthy of praise" (Phil. 4:8).

- Every once in a while during the day, I have to stop and marvel at the greatness of God.

Who has been winning the battle in your mind? What areas do you need to strengthen?

_____

_____

_____

Now turn to the battleground of your heart. Here are some tip-offs that Satan is on the move.

- I worry about receiving the recognition I deserve.

- I get peeved at others who don't serve the Lord like I do.

- I take great delight in others getting the punishment they deserve.

If Christ is making headway, these emotions will describe you:

- I'm glad to see others succeed in their ministries.

- I'm content with the position in life God has given me.

- My heart is tender toward the "least among you" (Luke 9:48).

How has the battle in your heart been going? What will help you soften your heart more?

_____

_____

_____

The next Living Insight addresses the battleground of the will.

Living Insights

Many hard-fought battles are waged in the will. Do any of these statements reveal to you that the enemy is gaining territory here?

- I desire to follow Christ . . . until I think about the hardships I might face.

- I desire to follow Christ . . . but all my responsibilities keep getting in the way.

- I desire to follow Christ . . . but first I have a few other things I'd like to do.

Christ, on the other hand, is winning this war if this single statement is true: Regardless of the consequences, I will follow Him.

Describe the battle in your will. Is anything keeping you from resolutely setting your face toward Him? If so, what is it?

_____

_____

_____

_____

_____

If you haven't done so, won't you make a commitment to Him right now?

No joy on earth is equal to the bliss of being all taken up with love to Christ. If I had my choice of all the lives that I could live, I certainly would not choose to be an emperor, nor to be a millionaire, nor to be a philosopher, for power and wealth and knowledge bring with them sorrow. But I would choose to have nothing to do but to love my Lord Jesus—nothing, I mean, but to do all things for his sake, and out of love to him.[4]

---

4. Charles Spurgeon, as quoted in *Spurgeon at His Best*, comp. Tom Carter (Grand Rapids, Mich.: Baker Book House, 1988), p. 123.

Chapter 14

PLAIN TALK TO ALL
IN MINISTRY

Luke 10:1–16

How would you describe the perfect pastor? One writer, with tongue in cheek, gives us the following sketch.

> After hundreds of years, a model preacher has been found to suit everyone. He preaches exactly 20 minutes and then sits down. He condemns sin, but never hurts anyone's feelings.
>
> He works from 8 a.m. to 10 p.m. in every type of work from preaching to custodial service. . . .
>
> He is 26 years old and has been preaching for 30 years. He is tall and short, thin and heavyset, and handsome. He has one brown eye and one blue, hair parted down the middle, left side dark and straight, the right brown and wavy.
>
> He has a burning desire to work with teenagers, and spends all his time with older folks. He smiles all the time with a straight face because he has a sense of humor that keeps him seriously dedicated to his work. He makes 15 calls a day on church members, spends all his time evangelizing the un-churched, and is never out of his office.[1]

What a crazy picture! Yet, frustratingly, that is the sort of impossible mold many church members try to force upon their pastors.

God doesn't expect leaders to be everything to everyone. His list of ideals is much shorter than ours. From Jesus' words in the first section of Luke 10, as He commissions a group of leaders for ministry, we can discern a few of His criteria.

---

1. From *Christian Beacon*, as quoted in *Encyclopedia of 7,700 Illustrations: Signs of the Times*, comp. Paul Lee Tan (n.p.: Assurance Publishers, 1979), p. 983.

A Little Contextual Background to Begin With

Having "resolutely set His face to go to Jerusalem" (9:51), Jesus is accelerating His training program. As Luke 10 begins, the Master is preparing more of His followers—beyond just the Twelve—to carry on the ministry after He is gone.

The People Who Are Sent

> Now after this the Lord appointed seventy others, and sent them two and two ahead of Him to every city and place where He Himself was going to come. (v. 1)

Jesus recruits seventy additional soldiers for frontline ministry. We're not told their names or how He selects them, but we do know that when the Captain announces their number, they come right away. They are Christ's minutemen, living out His challenge—"Let him deny himself, and take up his cross daily, and follow Me" (9:23).

By sending His soldiers out "two and two," Jesus reminds us that partnership is essential in the ministry. Two witnesses have greater credibility, and should trouble arise, two people can protect themselves better than one alone can protect himself.

The Places They Are Sent to Minister To

Where does Jesus send them? "To every city and place where He Himself was going to come." He alone decided their itinerary.

When we sign up with Jesus, we say yes to Him, not to a certain location. We can't imagine one of the seventy saying, "Gee, Lord, Jerusalem's OK, but I was really hoping for sunny Jericho." If He's truly Lord of our life, then we're willing to go anywhere there's work to be done . . . and in this world, there's *plenty* of work to be done.

> And He was saying to them, "The harvest is plentiful, but the laborers are few; therefore beseech the Lord of the harvest to send out laborers into His harvest." (10:2)

Notice two crucial points in this verse. First, Jesus calls us "laborers." No farmer gathers in the harvest while sitting in the porch swing sipping iced tea. Neither should a Christian worker expect to win souls for Christ without rolling up his or her sleeves and toiling in the fields.

And second, it is "His harvest." God alone is "the Lord of the harvest." We're not working with our flock, but *God's* flock. We're not serving our people, but *His* people. We're not carrying out our plan, but *His* plan. To His name goes the glory, and in His capable hands lie the results.

Sound Advice for Ministry in Any Generation

To His laborers Jesus gives the following advice, which we can categorize into five guidelines.[2]

Go God's Way, Not the World's Way

The first guideline has to do with the Person sending us.

> "Go your ways; behold, I send you out as lambs in the midst of wolves." (v. 3)

"Behold, *I* send you," Jesus says. We go at His command and by His will. His word of direction forms the firm foundation for our path. Even so, perils abound. We are sent as "lambs in the midst of wolves." Our teeth are not as sharp as our enemy's, but we're far from helpless. We depend on the Good Shepherd, who has sent us and will guard us, and we walk in the strength of His might.

Trusting Him, we're free to travel light. As verse 4 says,

> "Carry no purse, no bag, no shoes; and greet no one on the way."

Our survival depends on the Lord, not on things nor on people we meet along the way. In Jesus' culture, greetings were lengthy and more like visits, which could really eat away at a person's time, energy, and focus. Basically, Jesus is saying, "Don't live cluttered lives or get so caught up in the social whirl that your spiritual call is forgotten. Instead, stay centered on Me and My message."

Deliver God's Message, Not Man's

In the next verses, Jesus tells us the contents of His message.

> "And whatever house you enter, first say, 'Peace be to this house.' And if a man of peace is there, your peace will rest upon him; but if not, it will return to you." (vv. 5–6)

---

2. Much of what Jesus says in these verses resembles the commands He gave the disciples in Luke 9. Whether for the Twelve, the seventy, or us today, Jesus' guidelines remain the same.

What should be the first word on the lips of those who represent Christ? "Peace." Some ministers, however, stir up storm clouds of controversy and conflict wherever they go. Setting a doctrinal chip on their shoulder, they dare anyone to knock if off and start a fight. But Jesus says to bring a word of peace.

He also tells the seventy to say, "The kingdom of God has come near to you" (v. 9b). A minister's heart must beat with the message of God's kingdom, namely, His right to rule our lives. To water down that message for the sake of pleasing self-serving people is to dilute the life-changing power of the gospel. Never be ashamed to proclaim Jesus as Lord.

Model Contentment, Not Greed or Restlessness

When our message is welcomed, the next guideline shows us how to respond.

> "And stay in that house, eating and drinking what they give you; for the laborer is worthy of his wages. Do not keep moving from house to house. And whatever city you enter, and they receive you, eat what is set before you; and heal those in it who are sick." (vv. 7–9a)

Two exhortations flow from these verses. First, stay where you are; second, accept what you get. It takes time for a pastor to build trust and respect with a congregation. By always searching for greener pastorates, many ministers have bought into the philosophy of a greedy and restless world. We need pastors who model contentment, with both their location and their salary.

At the same time, congregations must be willing to pay their pastors a fair wage. "The laborer is worthy of his wages," Jesus says. But some churches respond, "We need to keep him humble, so we'll keep him broke." An attitude like that destroys a pastor's chances of modeling real contentment.

Minister with Heavenly Assurance, Not Earthly Fear

What if our message is not received? Jesus addresses that situation too.

> "But whatever city you enter and they do not receive you, go out into its streets and say, 'Even the dust of your city which clings to our feet, we wipe off in

protest against you; yet be sure of this, that the kingdom of God has come near.' I say to you, it will be more tolerable in that day for Sodom, than for that city. Woe to you, Chorazin! Woe to you, Bethsaida! For if the miracles had been performed in Tyre and Sidon which occurred in you, they would have repented long ago, sitting in sackcloth and ashes. But it will be more tolerable for Tyre and Sidon in the judgment, than for you. And you, Capernaum, will not be exalted to heaven, will you? You will be brought down to Hades!" (vv. 10–15)

God doesn't expect ministers to mete out His judgment. He'll take care of places like Chorazin and Bethsaida and Capernaum— places where the people turned up their noses at the offer of God's kingdom. The point is this: Don't take it personally when people reject God's message. He's the One they're criticizing. Shake the harsh words off your feet like dust, and move to a more receptive place of ministry.

Focus on Christ, Not Self

The guideline that appears last, but is foremost in importance, pertains to our focus.

"The one who listens to you listens to Me, and the one who rejects you rejects Me; and he who rejects Me rejects the One who sent Me." (v. 16)

When people listen to us, it's Christ they're really hearing. When people reject us, it's Christ they're really turning down. No doubt, Christian leaders are lightning rods in the church, but if we can keep our focus on Him, the flashes of praise and criticism that light up our sky will go right through us to Him. Keeping our eyes on Christ will protect us from both the pride of flattery and the pain of rejection.

Some Concluding Bits of Counsel

To close, let's bundle our thoughts into two easy loads that are light enough to carry wherever we go. One is for ministers; the other, for people being ministered to.

First, *to all who minister: be faithful to Him who called you.* The sirens of success can lure you away from your calling. Don't swerve to the left. Don't swerve to the right. Don't give in or give up. Stay faithful.

Second, *to all who are ministered to: be accountable to those who serve you.* God gave us our pastors to help us grow more like Christ. But they can't get close to us unless we let them. Invite your pastor into your life. Let your house be one that your minister can enter in a spirit of peace.

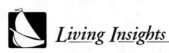 *Living Insights*

For Those in the Ministry

You know that one person can't be everywhere, do everything, and please everyone. But there's something inside you that says, "I can do it. I can be the perfect pastor." If you've been listening to that driving voice, where do you think it comes from?

_____

_____

_____

God's idea of "perfect" for you is far different than people's idea of perfection. The world adds up our appearance, accomplishments, and influence to total our success. God tosses out the numbers and looks at our hearts.

Take a moment to examine your heart as you think about the five guidelines from the lesson.

Are you going God's way, rather than the world's way—particularly concerning your definition of success?

_____

_____

_____

What message have you been proclaiming—God's or man's? Does it elevate Christ or self?

_____

_____

_____

Are you content?

_____

_____

_____

How are you handling criticism? Have you been able to shake
the dust off your feet when necessary?

_____

_____

_____

Where's your focus when praised? When rejected?

_____

_____

_____

We highly recommend that you read Kent and Barbara Hughes'
book *Liberating Ministry from the Success Syndrome*. Take Kent's
words to heart, won't you?

> As Barbara and I searched the Scriptures, we
> found no place where it says that God's servants are
> called to be *successful*. Rather, we discovered our call
> is to be *faithful*.[3]

 Living Insights STUDY TWO

For Those Ministered To

Pastors often feel like ducks in a religious shooting gallery—
always vulnerable, always different, always being fired at. But God
didn't call pastors to be the targets of our frustrations; He called
them as guides, to help us find our way to an understanding of

_____

3. Kent and Barbara Hughes, *Liberating Ministry from the Success Syndrome* (Wheaton, Ill.:
Tyndale House Publishers, 1987), p. 35.

ourselves, our world, and our Creator. We haven't arrived yet, and neither have they. We're all stumbling along together.

Kent and Barbara Hughes have suggested a few ways that we can encourage our pastors. The more we support our leaders, the clearer their vision will be as they lead us toward Christ.

- "First, you can encourage your pastor by living biblically successful lives yourselves."

- "Second, encourage your pastor by your personal commitment to help him know true success."

- "Third, encourage your pastor by not expecting (or allowing) him to be involved in everything."

- "Fourth, encourage your pastor by providing adequately for him and his family."

- "Fifth, encourage your pastor by loving his family."

- "Sixth, encourage your pastor by treating him with respect."[4]

How can you put one or two of these suggestions into practice this week?

_____

_____

_____

_____

_____

_____

4. Hughes, *Liberating Ministry,* pp. 189–94.

Chapter 15

JOYFUL REUNION—
INSIGHTFUL RESPONSE
Luke 10:17–24

To the cheers of the crowd and the clicking of news cameras, the lone sailor shoves off for a round-the-world voyage. The anticipation of a thousand new adventures fills his eyes. For months he has been preparing himself for this moment. The boat is fully trimmed and fitted. The wind is favorable. The sails flutter and snap to attention as the craft bravely glides out of the harbor and into the open sea.

There's something thrilling about the start of a new journey—whether a sea voyage, a marriage, or a ministry. At our backs is a breeze of hope; optimism fills our sails. We can conquer the world!

So thought the seventy Jesus had sent out on their first ministry adventure. Jesus had primed their hearts with courage and faith, and they were brimming with great expectations. But how would their idealism fare when tested in the harsh winds of reality? Would they return with the same spark in their eyes and energy in their steps?

The Return of Seventy "Ministers"

We don't know how long the seventy ministers were gone, where they went, or how people responded. But we do know the spirit in which they came home.

What They Reported

> And the seventy returned with joy, saying, "Lord, even the demons are subject to us in Your name." (Luke 10:17)

What storm could have been more frightening than a shivering encounter with a demon? Yet Christ's power in them overcame even this spiritual gale. Jesus hadn't told them, as He had told the apostles, that He had given them authority over evil spirits (see 9:1). What a joyful surprise it was to discover that He had provided everything they needed—and more.

How Jesus Responded

Jesus beamed as they shared their exploits with Him, because He knew more about their success than they realized. While they battled demons, He "was watching Satan fall from heaven like lightning" (10:18). In other words, as the seventy exercised His power on earth, Jesus knew in His spirit that they were shaking Satan's authority over the earth. God was using their ministries to defeat the Evil One. What could be more exciting than that?

> "Behold, I have given you authority to tread upon serpents and scorpions, and over all the power of the enemy, and nothing shall injure you. Nevertheless do not rejoice in this, that the spirits are subject to you, but rejoice that your names are recorded in heaven." (vv. 19–20)

Jesus is using figurative language here.[1] In talking about serpents and scorpions and by saying "nothing shall injure you," He doesn't mean that we're invincible. He means that we don't need to fear Satan—or people—who might try to poison the message of Christ. "Greater is He who is in you," John reminds us, "than he who is in the world" (1 John 4:4).

But as thrilling as it was for the seventy to conquer demons in Jesus' name, how much more joy there was in knowing that their names had been "recorded in heaven." The Greek word for *recorded* was the word used when people were enrolled on the official city lists "as citizens possessing the full privileges of the commonwealth."[2] By pointing out their citizenship in heaven, Jesus was helping the seventy focus on the security of their relationship with God. Feelings of power and spiritual highs come and go, but the anchor that holds us fast is the joyful assurance of eternal life with Christ.

What We Learn from This

Rather than rush ahead to the next insights in this passage, let's pause to reflect on some of what we've learned so far.

---

1. With tragic results, some Christians have taken this verse to mean literally that Christ will spare them from all harm. In the name of faith, they allow snakes and scorpions to bite them, but that is more presumption than faith. Jesus clearly said, "You shall not put the Lord your God to the test" (Luke 4:12).

2. Plummer, as quoted by Archibald Thomas Robertson, *Word Pictures in the New Testament* (Grand Rapids, Mich.: Baker Book House, 1930), vol. 2, p. 149.

First, how easy it is to get sidetracked, to allow the good of this life to overshadow the best that is to come. Displaying power over Satan is of temporal value. Of eternal benefit is Christ's power over death. Let's not focus on the temporal so much that we miss the eternal.

Second, while we have nothing to fear from Satan, we have everything to lose by choosing the wrong priorities. Remember Simon, the sorcerer in the book of Acts, who tried to buy the Spirit's power? Peter rebuked him because his heart was "not right before God" (Acts 8:21). Like Simon, we hear dramatic stories of spiritual power in people's lives, and we yearn for the spectacular. Yet what God yearns for is our tender, childlike faith in Him (compare Matt. 7:22–23).

So if you have trusted Christ for your salvation, rejoice! Don't discount what you have. No spiritual power can compare to the thrill of eternal life.

The Reaction of Jesus

As Jesus saw the lives of the seventy shining with God's power and presence, He knew redemption's plan was unfolding just as it was promised. A fountain of praise burst from His heart.

His Prayer before the Father

> At that very time He rejoiced greatly in the Holy Spirit, and said, "I praise Thee, O Father, Lord of heaven and earth, that Thou didst hide these things from the wise and intelligent and didst reveal them to babes. Yes, Father, for thus it was well-pleasing in Thy sight." (Luke 10:21)

The Son marveled at how His Father selected these "babes" as vessels for His truth instead of all the superior minds in palaces and universities. That's the way God is. When Jesus was born, the Father didn't pour the news into the porcelain vases of royalty or the well-crafted jars of the intelligentsia; He sent His angels to the shepherds in the field (see 2:8–20), the common clay pots of this world.

Why does God choose to place His treasure in ordinary lives? The apostle Paul gives us an answer. After trying to explain God's truth to the world's greatest philosophers and getting rebuffed, he wrote to the Corinthians,

> For the word of the cross is to those who are

perishing foolishness, but to us who are being saved
it is the power of God. For it is written,

"I will destroy the wisdom of the wise,
And the cleverness of the clever I will set aside."

Where is the wise man? Where is the scribe? Where
is the debater of this age? Has not God made foolish
the wisdom of the world? (1 Cor. 1:18–20)

Many people of great learning become so impressed with their
own intellects that they will not receive the simple truth of God's
revelation. Thinking they are already wise, they close their minds
to God's wisdom. So God calls "not many wise according to the
flesh, not many mighty, not many noble" (v. 26). In other words,
He calls us. Why?

That no man should boast before God. (v. 29)

We can't put our thumbs in our suspenders and proudly announce that we've earned eternal life. All of us must humbly hang
on to Christ's coattails to get into the kingdom of God.

His Statement to the Seventy

In Luke 10:22, Jesus appears to shift from talking to His Father
to talking to the seventy.

"All things have been handed over to Me by My
Father, and no one knows who the Son is except
the Father, and who the Father is except the Son,
and anyone to whom the Son wills to reveal Him."

How favored we are that Christ has chosen to reveal the Father
to us. Without Jesus, we would be left on our own to find God, and
most certainly, we would fail. By His grace, though, He chooses us
not because of our IQ or noble standing but according to His will.

His Blessings on the Disciples

And turning to the disciples, He said privately,
"Blessed are the eyes which see the things you see,
for I say to you, that many prophets and kings wished
to see the things which you see, and did not see
them, and to hear the things which you hear, and
did not hear them." (vv. 23–24)

Luke includes this private word between Jesus and the Twelve, called a "beatitude of privilege," a blessing specifically for them. Out of the millions and millions of people throughout history, these twelve men were selected to see the Son of God up close, to perform miracles in His name, to hear His most intimate words. These are things about which the greatest of prophets and kings only dreamed.

We are privileged as well, because we can personally know the incarnate Christ. For this reason, the poorest disciple of Jesus is richer by far than the wealthiest king of this world.

What We Learn from This

How are you doing on your journey as a disciple? Perhaps you began well. You launched out like the seventy, with a heart overflowing with zeal and enthusiasm. But maybe the harsh winds of the world have given you a beating. Blown off course, you've lost sight of what a disciple is supposed to do.

Rather than resign in discouragement, re-sign your pledge to Christ in the faith that He will help you see His truth, hear His truth, believe His truth, and obey His truth. Rediscover the privileges of being a follower of Christ.

 Living Insights STUDY ONE

Sometimes we have difficulty rejoicing that our names are written in heaven. The reason is, we're afraid. We're afraid that God will scratch our names off the list at the slightest sinful provocation. We're afraid our faith is too weak, that our names will fade and disappear.

Do you ever battle those fears? When do they assault you most?

_____

_____

_____

A couple of insights into Luke 10:20 may help settle your turmoil. First, Christ commands us to "rejoice." He doesn't say, "Be on guard!" or, "Watch yourselves! Your names are recorded now, but they could be rubbed out at any time." We wouldn't have much to rejoice about if that was the case.

Also, the Greek word for *recorded* is passive, meaning it has been done for us. We do not enroll ourselves—Christ writes our names in His "Lamb's book of life" (Rev. 21:27). He keeps our place in heaven. And once He gives eternal life, we can feel secure in His promise because of who He is. He said,

> "My sheep hear My voice, and I know them, and they follow Me; and I give eternal life to them, and they shall never perish; and no one shall snatch them out of My hand." (John 10:27–28)

Add to this tremendous promise what the following verses have to say about your security in Christ.

Ephesians 1:13–14 _____

_____

Philippians 3:20–21 _____

_____

1 John 5:11–13 _____

_____

Rejoice! Based on His death and resurrection, Christ has bought you, cleansed you, enrolled you in heaven, and taken you as His own.

 Living Insights

Every night, Joe walked through the luxurious office on the top floor of the downtown high-rise to empty the president's trash. Every night, he polished the counters and vacuumed the carpet. And every night, he dreamed of what it would be like to sit behind that elegant mahogany desk.

What power he would have. Millions of dollars would be at his command. When he barked orders, people in offices on ten floors would jump. Everyone would call him "Sir."

One night, he dared himself to do it. He peeked into the hallway. Nobody. He scanned the spacious office to check for cameras. None. Quietly, he rolled back the thronelike chair, and, holding his breath, he eased into the Corinthian leather.

Joe was boss of the world.

When the seventy healed the sick and cast out demons in Jesus' name, they must have felt like Joe, sitting in the president's chair. Great power was at their fingertips . . . yet none of it was their own. It was all Christ's.

Are you ever tempted to claim Christ's power as your own? To take the credit for answered prayer or changed lives or biblical insights you share with others? In what ways?

_____

_____

_____

Sitting in Christ's chair, we tend to get carried away. We tend to let His powers go to our heads. "Do not rejoice in this," Jesus warned, "that the spirits are subject to you, but rejoice that your names are recorded in heaven" (Luke 10:20).

One day, the Boss will return. Keep your focus on that day and the glories to follow. It will help you remember whose chair you're sitting in.

Chapter 16

WHAT ABOUT MY NEIGHBOR'S NEIGHBOR?

Luke 10:25–37

Sometimes a return to basics is absolutely necessary.

When Vince Lombardi's Green Bay Packers were at their zenith, they were practically unbeatable. But they got overconfident and lost what should have been an easy game against the Chicago Bears on Soldier Field. Their coach was livid. When their plane landed in frozen-over Green Bay, Lombardi bused them directly to Lambeau Field and had them don their still-sweaty gear from the game. Then began a nightlong practice session, kicked off with the coach's pointed words: "Gentlemen, this is a football!"

How basic can you get? It's like telling the Boston Symphony Orchestra, "Ladies and gentlemen, this is a half note." Or informing a librarian, "This is a book." Yet when people begin to drift off track, we need to return to the fundamentals—and for Christians, that means caring for our neighbor.

What a football is to a team, what a half note is to a symphony, what a book is to a librarian, a neighbor is to a Christian. How can we honestly say we're interested in reaching the world for Christ if we're not concerned with reaching the person next door, in the office across the way, or in the shop down the street?

So let's join our Head Coach in Luke 10, where Jesus gets us back to basics: "Christian, this is a neighbor!"

Addressing the Heart of the Issue

Rather than preach about it, Jesus masterfully pictures this thought for us in the moving story of the Good Samaritan. It is set in the context of a conversation He is having with a Jewish lawyer, who has decided to put Jesus to the test.

This chapter has been adapted from "Is My Neighbor Really Lost?" in the study guide *Questions Christians Ask*, coauthored by David Lien, from the Bible-teaching ministry of Charles R. Swindoll (Fullerton, Calif.: Insight for Living, 1989), pp. 34–38.

130

Dialogue: A Lawyer and Jesus

The legal expert begins by asking a question.

> And behold, a certain lawyer stood up and put Him to the test, saying, "Teacher, what shall I do to inherit eternal life?" (v. 25)

Turning the test around, Jesus answers the man with another question.

> "What is written in the Law? How does it read to you?" (v. 26)

William Barclay points out the subtlety in Jesus' response:

> Strict orthodox Jews wore round their wrists little leather boxes called phylacteries, which contained certain passages of scripture—*Exodus* 13:1–10; 11–16; *Deuteronomy* 6:4–9; 11:13–20. . . . So Jesus said to the scribe, "Look at the phylactery on your own wrist and it will answer your question."[1]

Dutifully, the lawyer quotes the Scripture he knows so well:

> "You shall love the Lord your God with all your heart, and with all your soul, and with all your strength, and with all your mind; and your neighbor as yourself." (v. 27)

Jesus congratulates him for his right answer, but He also challenges the lawyer to go beyond Scripture memory and start putting his knowledge into action.

> And He said to him, "You have answered correctly; do this, and you will live." (v. 28)

Today, we would say, "You got it. Now get at it!" As far as Jesus was concerned, the case was closed.

The lawyer, however, didn't care for the incriminating verdict. Reluctant to leave the scene bearing the burden of the argument, he shifts it back to Jesus and tries to squirm off the hook of responsibility by quibbling over the meaning of a word.

---

1. William Barclay, *The Gospel of Luke*, rev. ed., The Daily Study Bible Series (Philadelphia, Pa.: Westminster Press, 1975), p. 140.

But wishing to justify himself, he said to Jesus, "And who is my neighbor?" (v. 29)

Some rabbis of the day, according to Barclay, "confined the word *neighbour* to their *fellow Jews*."[2] Sidestepping the definitions debate, Jesus instead told a story that would explain His meaning beyond a doubt.

Monologue: Jesus and a Story

Jesus replied and said, "A certain man was going down from Jerusalem to Jericho; and he fell among robbers, and they stripped him and beat him, and went off leaving him half dead." (v. 30)

Jesus' story is about a man in need—a man who had taken a treacherous journey from Jerusalem to Jericho, where the way was craggy and steep and the altitude dropped thirty-six hundred feet over a distance of twenty miles. Robbers loved that lonely stretch of road. They could mug, murder, and rape without fear of intervention. Called "The Bloody Way," it was a threatening and dangerous road for a person traveling alone.[3]

As Jesus continues, the drama heightens. He introduces two religious men into His story, drawing the pious lawyer into a net of emotional identification.

"And by chance a certain priest was going down on that road, and when he saw him, he passed by on the other side. And likewise a Levite also, when he came to the place and saw him, passed by on the other side." (vv. 31–32)

These two men deliberately avoided the bleeding man lying crumpled in the dirt. The first was a priest of Jerusalem's temple, a man whose life was consecrated to the things of God. The second, a Levite, was an assistant to the first. Both men, religious professionals, saw the man but ignored the need.

James has something to say about this kind of proficient, heartless religion: it's useless!

If a brother or sister is without clothing and in need

2. Barclay, *The Gospel of Luke*, p. 140.
3. Barclay, *The Gospel of Luke*, pp. 138–39.

of daily food, and one of you says to them, "Go in peace, be warmed and be filled," and yet you do not give them what is necessary for their body, what use is that? Even so faith, if it has no works, is dead, being by itself. (James 2:15–17)

And according to John, if we truly loved God, we'd open our hearts and show love toward others also.

We know love by this, that He laid down His life for us; and we ought to lay down our lives for the brethren. But whoever has the world's goods, and beholds his brother in need and closes his heart against him, how does the love of God abide in him? Little children, let us not love with word or with tongue, but in deed and truth. (1 John 3:16–18)

Jesus next contrasts the response of the two religious men with that of another traveler—a man with unusual understanding and compassion.

"But a certain Samaritan, who was on a journey, came upon him; and when he saw him, he felt compassion, and came to him, and bandaged up his wounds, pouring oil and wine on them; and he put him on his own beast, and brought him to an inn, and took care of him. And on the next day he took out two denarii and gave them to the innkeeper and said, 'Take care of him; and whatever more you spend, when I return, I will repay you.'" (Luke 10:33–35)

Samaritans were Jews whose ancestors come from the northern ten tribes of Israel and who long ago had intermarried with the Assyrians. They held that Mount Gerizim, not Jerusalem, was the true place of worship. For these reasons, the full-blooded Jews despised the Samaritans and criticized their errant beliefs. Yet it was a Samaritan whose faith proved the most worthy.

Jesus says the Samaritan "felt compassion." He saw the same pitiful man lying in agony, but his heart churned within him so that he couldn't pass by without helping. That's the way compassion affects us. It stirs us; it troubles us; it keeps us awake at night until we do something.

Did you notice the lengths to which the Samaritan went to show love to the man?

- He came to him.

- He poured healing oil and wine on his wounds and bandaged them.

- He put him on his beast and brought him to an inn.

- He took care of him through the night.

- The next day, he made provisions for his recovery.

Unlike Jerusalem's religious elite, the Samaritan went the extra mile for this man in need. He was a good neighbor—which brings Jesus to the point of His story.

Question: The Story and a Neighbor

Jesus narrows His message to a single question, thrust like a spear to its mark—the lawyer's heart.

> "Which of these three do you think proved to be a neighbor to the man who fell into the robbers' hands?" And he said, "The one who showed mercy toward him." And Jesus said to him, "Go and do the same." (vv. 36–37)

The Lord deftly shifts the original question from, "Who is my neighbor?" to the more important question, "What kind of neighbor am I?" Like the lawyer, we often want to place the burden of responsibility on someone else's shoulders. Our degree of mercy depends on whether people fit the description of a worthy neighbor. But Jesus throws the burden back on us. The real issue is not, Is my neighbor really lost? But, Are we—our neighbor's neighbors— really saved? Are we really people of compassion who love the Lord our God with all our heart, soul, strength, and mind; who love our neighbors as ourselves and prove it in our actions?

Coming to Terms with the Truth

The answer to those questions depends on who we are and our desire to change, if necessary. The Samaritan was a compassionate person, so he saw the wounded man's brokenness and pain. As a result, he did something about it. The principle is this: Who we are determines what we see, and what we see determines what we do. One man writes with conviction,

> Compassion is not a snob gone slumming. . . . Did you ever take a *real* trip down inside the broken heart of a friend? To feel the sob of the soul—the raw, red crucible of emotional agony? To have this become almost as much yours as that of your soul-crushed neighbor? Then, to sit down with him—and silently weep? This is the beginning of compassion.[4]

Christianity doesn't get more basic than that. A caring, compassionate heart is absolutely essential to the message we have to share with the world. As another man has said, "Nobody cares how much you know—until they know how much you care."[5] People won't hear our words until they see Christ's love demonstrated in our outstretched hands.

 Living Insights STUDY ONE

How can we demonstrate Christ's love? Chuck Swindoll illustrates one practical way in a personal story that goes back to his days in seminary.

In his last year at school, several crises brought him into a dark period of depression. His wife, Cynthia, had had a miscarriage at five and a half months. Three months later his car was hit by a drunk driver, breaking the jaw of his young son, Curt, and deeply bruising Cynthia, who was pregnant again. The following seven months would have Cynthia bedridden, in and out of the hospital, threatened with losing the baby. During all this, her mom in Houston was slowly dying of breast cancer.

Chuck's family was hurting; he was without money or a car; and he faced an unknown future. He tells what happened one night after the accident while Cynthia was in the hospital, when he was feeling especially low.

Late one evening, after studying in the library till it

4. Jess Moody, as quoted in *Quotable Quotations*, comp. Lloyd Cory (Wheaton, Ill.: Scripture Press Publications, Victor Books, 1985), p. 76.

5. John Cassis, as quoted in *Quotable Quotations*, p. 52.

closed, I thought I would go find a professor who would put his arms around me, a man I had studied under, someone, any one of them that I had been learning from and following for three and a half years. I remember knocking on a door and no one answered, and walking a little further and no one answered. Finally, there [was] a light on. Somebody [was] there.

And, rather coolly, this man I had known for those years opened his door a crack. "Yes?" he stared at me. And when I saw his face, had I known it was him, I don't believe I would have disturbed him, because I knew when I saw him that he didn't have the capacity to understand. . . .

"Yes, Chuck. What do you want?"

I stood there and tears just ran from my eyes. And I could hear in his voice that he didn't want to talk to me. I said, "Am I disturbing you?"

"Yes, you're disturbing me. What do you want?" was his answer.

I said, "Nothing. I don't want anything."

He said, "Fine." Closed the door.

I needed somebody. I wanted somebody who would simply understand what it felt like. . . .

The next morning, while still trying to find my way through the labyrinth of my feelings and get up on my own feet from my depression and my fears of losing our baby and maybe even losing a wife—I didn't know—Howie Hendricks walked up to me and put his arms around me and won my heart and has won it to this day. And he understood [my confusion] as he told me of their miscarriage. And then I wanted to know what he knew, because I then knew how much he cared.[6]

Showing compassion can be as simple as putting an arm around someone and sharing their sorrow. All it takes is an ability to see the signs of pain, stop what we're doing, and open wide the door.

6. From Chuck Swindoll's sermon, "What about My Neighbor's Neighbor?" given at the First Evangelical Free Church of Fullerton, California, November 22, 1992.

Has someone been knocking on your door, looking for understanding and compassion? A child? A parent? A friend? Won't you be a good neighbor and let that person in?

 Living Insights

Congratulations! You've reached the midpoint of our journey through Luke. Imagine yourself halfway up a mountain, and take a moment to look back and see how far you've come. What an amazing display of scenes and events your path has passed through in the life of Christ!

Which ones have meant the most to you? Why?

_____

_____

_____

_____

How have they deepened your appreciation and love for Christ?

_____

_____

_____

What one truth can you carry with you as you travel on in the book of Luke?

_____

_____

_____

In the next volume of our series on Luke, we'll see Jesus setting His gaze on the Cross even more. Parables will become His main teaching tool; the disciples, His primary audience. The path Jesus follows will get narrower and narrower the closer He comes to the end. Are you ready for this next part of the journey? Then let's go—He is waiting for you.

BOOKS FOR PROBING FURTHER

Our forefathers have passed down to us no greater gift than the words of the Savior. Treasure them. Hold them to your heart, for they are life and peace and joy. Do you remember some of them from this study of Luke's gospel?

"Do not weep. . . . I say to you, arise!" (7:13–14)

"Your sins have been forgiven. . . . Your faith has saved you." (vv. 48, 50)

"Where is your faith?" (8:25)

"Who is the one who touched Me? . . . Go in peace." (vv. 45, 48)

"Do not be afraid. . . . Stop weeping. . . . Child, arise!" (vv. 50, 52, 54)

"Take nothing for your journey." (9:3)

"You give them something to eat!" (v. 13)

"Who do the multitudes say that I am? . . . Who do you say that I am?" (vv. 18, 20)

"The Son of Man must suffer. . . . If anyone wishes to come after Me, let him deny himself . . . take up his cross . . . and follow Me. . . . Whoever loses his life for My sake, he is the one who will save it." (vv. 22–24)

"He who is least among you, this is the one who is great." (v. 48)

"The Son of Man did not come to destroy men's lives, but to save them." (v. 56)

"The kingdom of God has come near to you." (10:9)

"Rejoice that your names are recorded in heaven." (v. 20)

"Blessed are the eyes which see the things you see."
(v. 23)

So deep, so vast, so powerful are Jesus' words. Who can measure their wealth? We can spend a lifetime uncovering their hidden riches.

To help you dig deeper into Jesus' truths of gold, we've provided you with a list of resources. Choose a tool and start mining! You're sure to strike it rich.

Gire, Ken. *Incredible Moments with the Savior.* Grand Rapids, Mich.: Zondervan Publishing House, 1990.

Griffiths, Michael. *The Example of Jesus.* The Jesus Library Series. Downers Grove, Ill.: InterVarsity Press, 1985.

Lucado, Max. *The Applause of Heaven.* Dallas, Tex.: Word Publishing, 1990.

McClung, Floyd. *Basic Discipleship.* Downers Grove, Ill.: InterVarsity Press, 1990.

Morris, Leon. *The Gospel according to St. Luke.* The Tyndale New Testament Commentaries Series. Grand Rapids, Mich.: William B. Eerdmans Publishing Co., 1974.

Sanders, J. Oswald. *The Incomparable Christ.* Revised and enlarged edition. Chicago, Ill.: Moody Press, 1971.

Sproul, R. C. *The Glory of Christ.* Wheaton, Ill.: Tyndale House Publishers, 1990.

Strauss, Richard L. *Growing More like Jesus.* Neptune, N.J.: Loizeaux, 1991.

White, John. *Magnificent Obsession: The Joy of Christian Commitment.* Revised edition. Downers Grove, Ill.: InterVarsity Press, 1990.

Some of these books may be out of print and available only through a library. For those currently available, please contact your local Christian bookstore. Books by Charles R. Swindoll may be obtained through Insight for Living. IFL also offers some books by other authors—please note the ordering information that follows and contact the office that serves you.

ORDERING INFORMATION

THE CONTINUATION OF SOMETHING GREAT
Cassette Tapes and Study Guide

This Bible study guide was designed to be used independently or in conjunction with the broadcast of Chuck Swindoll's taped messages which are listed below. If you would like to order cassette tapes or further copies of this study guide, please see the information given below and the order form provided at the end of this guide.

		U.S.	Canada
CSG	Study guide	$ 4.95 ea.	$ 6.50 ea.
CSGCS	Cassette series, includes all individual tapes, album cover, and one complimentary study guide	55.15	65.75
CSG 1–8	Individual cassettes, includes messages A and B	6.30 ea.	8.00 ea.

The prices are subject to change without notice.

CSG 1–A: *There Is Always Hope*—Luke 7:1–17
        B: *In Defense of a Doubter*—Luke 7:18–35

CSG 2–A: *Jesus at His Best*—Luke 7:36–50
        B: *Unseen yet Significant Contributors*—Luke 8:1–3

CSG 3–A: *Where Are You in This Picture?*—Luke 8:4–15
        B: *Hidden Secrets, Family Struggles, Stormy Seas*—Luke 8:16–25

CSG 4–A: *Freedom from Bondage*—Luke 8:26–39
        B: *Never Too Little . . . Never Too Lost*—Luke 8:40–56

CSG 5–A: *Secrets of a Lasting Ministry*—Luke 9:1–11
        B: *The Miracle Meal*—Luke 9:12–17

CSG 6–A: *A Shocking Agenda*—Luke 9:18–27
        B: *The Ultimate Close Encounter*—Luke 9:28–36

CSG 7–A: *Snapshots from an Amazing Album*—Luke 9:37–62
        B: *Plain Talk to All in Ministry*—Luke 10:1–16

CSG 8–A: *Joyful Reunion—Insightful Response*—Luke 10:17–24
        B: *What about My Neighbor's Neighbor?*—Luke 10:25–37

How to Order by Phone or FAX
(Credit card orders only)

United States: 1-800-772-8888 from 7:00 A.M. to 4:30 P.M., Pacific time, Monday through Friday
FAX (714) 575-5496 anytime, day or night

Canada: 1-800-663-7639, Vancouver residents call (604) 596-2910 from 8:00 A.M. to 5:00 P.M., Pacific time, Monday through Friday
FAX (604) 596-2975 anytime, day or night

Australia and the South Pacific: (03) 872-4606 or FAX (03) 874-8890 from 8:00 A.M. to 5:00 P.M., Monday through Friday

---

Other International Locations: call the Ordering Services Department in the United States at (714) 575-5000 during the hours listed above.

How to Order by Mail

United States
- Mail to: Ordering Services Department
  Insight for Living
  Post Office Box 69000
  Anaheim, CA 92817-0900
- Sales tax: California residents add 7.25%.
- Shipping: add 10% of the total order amount for first-class delivery. (Otherwise, allow four to six weeks for fourth-class delivery.)
- Payment: personal checks, money orders, credit cards (Visa, Master-Card, Discover Card, and American Express). No invoices or COD orders available.
- $10 fee for any returned check.

Canada
- Mail to: Insight for Living Ministries
  Post Office Box 2510
  Vancouver, BC V6B 3W7
- Sales tax: please add 7% GST. British Columbia residents also add 7% sales tax (on tapes or cassette series).
- Shipping: included in prices listed above.
- Payment: personal cheques, money orders, credit cards (Visa, Master-Card). No invoices or COD orders available.
- Delivery: approximately four weeks.

Australia and the South Pacific
- Mail to: Insight for Living, Inc.
    GPO Box 2823 EE
    Melbourne, Victoria 3001, Australia
- Shipping: add 25% to the total order.
- Delivery: approximately four to six weeks.
- Payment: personal checks payable in Australian funds, international money orders, or credit cards (Visa, MasterCard, and BankCard).

Other International Locations
- Mail to: Ordering Services Department
    Insight for Living
    Post Office Box 69000
    Anaheim, CA 92817-0900
- Shipping and delivery time: please see chart that follows.
- Payment: personal checks payable in U.S. funds, international money orders, or credit cards (Visa, MasterCard, and American Express).

Type of Shipping	Postage Cost	Delivery
Surface	10% of total order*	6 to 10 weeks
Airmail	25% of total order*	under 6 weeks

Use U.S. price as a base.

Our Guarantee

Your complete satisfaction is our top priority here at Insight for Living. If you're not completely satisfied with anything you order, please return it for full credit, a refund, or a replacement, as *you* prefer.

Insight for Living Catalog

The Insight for Living catalog features study guides, tapes, and books by a variety of Christian authors. To obtain a free copy, call us at the numbers listed above.

Order Form
United States, Australia, and Other International Locations
(Canadian residents please use order form on reverse side.)

CSGCS represents the entire *The Continuation of Something Great* series in a special album cover, while CSG 1–8 are the individual tapes included in the series. CSG represents this study guide, should you desire to order additional copies.

CSG	Study guide	$ 4.95 ea.
CSGCS	Cassette series, includes all individual tapes, album cover, and one complimentary study guide	55.15
CSG 1–8	Individual cassettes, includes messages A and B	6.30 ea.

Product Code	Product Description	Quantity	Unit Price	Total
			$	$
		Subtotal		
	California Residents—Sales Tax *Add 7.25% of subtotal.*			
	U.S. First-Class Shipping *For faster delivery, add 10% for postage and handling.*			
	Non-United States Residents *Australia add 25% for shipping and handling.* *All other locations: U.S. price plus 10% surface postage or 25% airmail.*			
	Gift to Insight for Living *Tax-deductible in the United States.*			
	Total Amount Due *Please do not send cash.*	$		

Prices are subject to change without notice.

Payment by: ❏ Check or money order payable to Insight for Living ❏ Credit card

(Circle one):   Visa   MasterCard   Discover Card   American Express   BankCard
(In Australia)

Number _____

Expiration Date _____   Signature _____
We cannot process your credit card purchase without your signature.

Name _____

Address _____

City _____   State _____

Zip Code _____   Country _____

Telephone (___) _____   Radio Station ____ ____ ____ ____
If questions arise concerning your order, we may need to contact you.

Mail this order form to the Ordering Services Department at one of these addresses:

Insight for Living
Post Office Box 69000, Anaheim, CA 92817-0900

Insight for Living, Inc.
GPO Box 2823 EE, Melbourne, VIC 3001, Australia

ECFA MEMBER

Order Form
Canadian Residents

(Residents of the United States, Australia, and other international locations, please use order form on reverse side.)

CSGCS represents the entire *The Continuation of Something Great* series in a special album cover, while CSG 1–8 are the individual tapes included in the series. CSG represents this study guide, should you desire to order additional copies.

CSG	Study guide	$ 6.50 ea.
CSGCS	Cassette series, includes all individual tapes, album cover, and one complimentary study guide	65.75
CSG 1–8	Individual cassettes, includes messages A and B	8.00 ea.

Product Code	Product Description	Quantity	Unit Price	Total
			$	$
		Subtotal		
		Add 7% GST		
	British Columbia Residents *Add 7% sales tax on individual tapes or cassette series.*			
	Gift to Insight for Living Ministries *Tax-deductible in Canada.*			
	Total Amount Due *Please do not send cash.*		$	

Prices are subject to change without notice.

Payment by: ☐ Check or money order payable to Insight for Living Ministries
☐ Credit card

(Circle one): Visa   MasterCard   Number _____

Expiration Date _____   Signature _____
We cannot process your credit card purchase without your signature.

Name _____

Address _____

City _____   Province _____

Postal Code _____   Country _____

Telephone (____) _____   Radio Station ____ ____ ____ ____
If questions arise concerning your order, we may need to contact you.

Mail this order form to the Ordering Services Department at the following address:

Insight for Living Ministries
Post Office Box 2510
Vancouver, BC, Canada V6B 3W7